TOXIC TORT

TOXIC TORT

Medical And Legal Elements

Third Edition

Ernest P. Chiodo, M.D., J.D., M.P.H., M.S., M.B.A., C.I.H.

Physician-Attorney
Diplomate of the American Board of Internal Medicine
Diplomate of the American Board of Preventive Medicine in Occupational Medicine
Diplomate of the American Board of Preventive Medicine in Public Health and General Preventive Medicine
Diplomate of the American Board of Industrial Hygiene as a Certified Industrial Hygienist in the Comprehensive Practice of Industrial Hygiene

To order additional copies of this book, contact:
Xlibris Corporation
1-888-795-4274
www.Xlibris.com
Orders@Xlibris.com
129826

CONTENTS

ABOUT THE CONTRIBUTORS 15

FOREWORD 17

INTRODUCTION 21

PART ONE

LEGAL CONSIDERATIONS

WARNING 25

CHAPTER ONE.. 27
WHAT IS TOXIC TORT LAW?

CHAPTER TWO... 29
PRACTICAL CONSIDERATIONS IN TOXIC TORT LAW

CHAPTER THREE 31
A PRIMER ON TOXIC TORT LAW

CHAPTER FOUR 53
CAUSATION IN TOXIC TORT LITIGATION

CHAPTER FIVE 58
DAMAGES IN TOXIC TORT LITIGATION

MEDICAL MONITORING DAMAGES 68

CHAPTER SEVEN 73
EXPERT WINTESSES

CHAPTER EIGHT.. 77
DAUBERT RULES LIMITING EXPERT WITNESS TESTIMONY

CHAPTER NINE 82
SOPHISTICATED USER DOCTRINE

CHAPTER TEN 84
WORKER'S COMPENSATION AS EXCLUSIVE REMEDY

CHAPTER NINE 86
INFORMATION GATHERING AND SELECTED FORMS

THE TOXIC TORT COMPLAINT 93

PART TWO

TECHNICAL ISSUES

MATHEMATICS 103

STATISTICS 104

TOXICOLOGY 107

EPIDEMIOLOGY 109

LUNG DISEASE 112

PART THREE

SPECIFIC TOXINS

ACROLEIN 121

ANTIMONY 122

ARSENIC 123

ASBESTOS 124

BARIUM 125

BENZENE 126

BERYLLIUM 127

CADMIUM 128

CARBON MONOXIDE 129

CARBON TETRACHLORIDE 130

CHLOROFORM 131

CHROMATED COPPER ARSENATE (CCA) 132

CHROMIUM 133

COBALT 134

CYANIDE 135

DIBROMOCHLOROPROPANE 136

DICHLORODIPHENYLTRICHLOROETHANE (DDT) 137

2,3,7,8-TETRACHLORODIBENZO-p-DIOXIN (DIOXIN) 138

FORMALDEHYDE 139

LEAD 140

MANGANESE 141

MERCURY 142

MOLDS... 143

OSMIUM 144

PHOSPHORUS... 145

PLATINUM... 146

POLYCHLORINATED BIPHENYLS (PCBs) 147

RADIUM... 148

RADON... 149

SILICA 150

VANADIUM.. 151

PART FOUR

CASE STUDIES

CASE ONE 157
LUNG CANCER, ASBESTOS EXPOSURE
AND CIGARETTE SMOKING

CASE TWO 159
PULMONARY FIBROSIS, METAL DUST,
AND CIGARETTE SMOKING

CASE THREE... 161
CHEMICAL INDUCED LUNG DISEASE

CASE FOUR... 165
ALLEGED POST SURGICAL HEPATITIS

CASE FIVE 167
RADIUM EXPOSURE

CASE SIX 171
A CASE OF LIGHTNING AND CARPAL TUNNEL SYNDROME

BIBLIOGRAPHY 173

DEDICATION

To

Our Parents
Who gave us life and wisdom

Nothing is a poison and everything is a poison,
it is only a matter of the dose.

Paracelsus

ABOUT THE CONTRIBUTORS

ERNEST P. CHIODO

Ernest P. Chiodo, M.D., J.D., M.P.H., M.S., M.B.A., C.I.H. is a physician, attorney, industrial hygienist, industrial toxicologist and biomedical engineer licensed to practice medicine in New York, Michigan, and Illinois as well as law in Michigan and Illinois. Dr. Chiodo received his Medical Degree (M.D.) from Wayne State University School of Medicine, his Juris Doctor (J.D.) from Wayne State University Law School, his Master of Public Health (M.P.H.) from Harvard University School of Public Health, his Master of Science in Biomedical Engineering (M.S.) from Wayne State University, his Master of Science in Threat Response Management (biological, chemical, and radiological defense) from the University of Chicago, his Master of Science in Occupational and Environmental Health Sciences with Specialization in Industrial Toxicology from Wayne State University, and his Master of Business Administration with a concentration in economics from the University of Chicago. He is board certified in the medical specialties of Internal Medicine, Occupational Medicine, and Public Health and General Preventive Medicine. Public Health and General Preventive Medicine is the medical specialty focused on epidemiology. He is also certified in the engineering and public health discipline of industrial hygiene by the American Board of Industrial Hygiene as a Certified Industrial Hygienist (C.I.H.) in the comprehensive practice of industrial hygiene. He has served as the President of the Michigan Industrial Hygiene Society. Dr. Chiodo is an assistant clinical professor of family medicine and public health at Wayne State University School of Medicine and has clinical privileges in the Henry Ford Health System. He has served as an Adjunct Professor of Industrial Hygiene and Industrial Toxicology at Wayne State University. He has also served as the Medical Director of the City of Detroit and of the Detroit Health Department and was the chief physician responsible for measures designed to protect the public health of over one million persons living or working in the City of Detroit. He has also served as the Medical Director of the pension boards of the City of Lansing, Michigan which is the capital city of the State of Michigan. In addition, he has served as the medical advisor to the final appeals committee of Jefferson Pilot Financial disability insurance carrier.

Dr. Chiodo serves as the Chairman of the Environmental Litigation and Administrative Practice Committee of the Environmental Law Section of the State Bar of Michigan. He also serves as an Adjunct Professor of Law at John Marshall Law School and Loyola University Law School in Chicago.

MARK ROULEAU

Mark Rouleau is a prominent member of the plaintiff's bar in Illinois concentrating in catastrophic injuries. He has published numerous articles on various aspects of the law including proof of facts regarding about the unreliability of the Horizontal Gaze Nystagmus (HGN) test for use in determining blood alcohol concentrations (BAC). Mark also prepared the practice tips to the 2012 Lexis/Nexus Illinois Civil Procedure (Parness) Supplement ch. 19-25. He is currently a member of the ISBA Civil Practice Section and is a former Chair of the Tort Section Council as well as the Young Lawyers Division where he also served as the editor of its newsletter. Mark served on the ISBA Task Force on Allocation of Judges, and the ISBA Task Force on Certification. He was a participant of the Illinois Legal Education Conclave, the ISBA Organized Bar Leadership Conference, and was an ISBA delegate to several ABA—YLD conventions. He is a frequent author of articles and speaker at continuing legal education seminars.

DAN BREEN

Dan Breen is a plaintiff's attorney and has litigated numerous toxic exposure cases. Dan is a regular contributor to the Illinois State Bar Association publication, "The Bottom Line" and also writes occasionally for the blog "Solo in Chicago". Dan is actively affiliated with the Illinois State Bar Association Standing Committee on Law Office Management and Economics, the John Marshall Law School Alumni Board, the Chicago Bar Association, Illinois Association of Independent Attorneys, Chicago Council on Global Affairs, and the Illinois Trial Lawyers Association. Dan has tried numerous cases to verdict and looks forward to many more.

FOREWORD

By

Donnelly W. Hadden, J.D.

Former Chairman of the Environmental Law Section of the State Bar of Michigan

This is a book about poisons and lawsuits. We live in a world of chemicals; indeed, we are ourselves made of chemicals. Many chemicals are benign and are essential to human life. However, some chemicals are poisonous to mankind. This has always been the case. There are poisons in nature including the hemlock plant, oleander, some mushrooms, locoweed, and many other types of flora. Some animals produce venom dangerous to humans. There are toxic minerals and elements, such as lead, phosphorus, and quicklime. These kinds of toxins have been known since the memory of man runneth not to the contrary. Many more recently developed useful common substances are toxic if misused. Gasoline, which was first refined from crude oil in commercial quantities a little more than a century ago, is a chemical that is necessary to the function of our modern society. It is ubiquitous. It is also toxic if swallowed. The same is true of many common products including ammonia and paint thinner.

With many toxic substances it is not so much the act of ingesting them that produces toxicity, rather it is the amount taken in. Grain alcohol is a very popular poison. Taken in small quantities it produces a state of blissful relaxation known to many adults. Consumption of larger quantities causes intoxication with the drinker suffering from ethyl alcohol poisoning. Continued ingestion can cause death. So, it is not only the type of toxic chemical that one is exposed to that is important, but also the amount of the chemical. The "dosage" as it is referred to in pharmacological terms is important. I have a friend who is an anesthesiologist that has testified on behalf of some of my clients. During the course of qualifying him as an expert on direct examination he likes me to ask him the following question: "Doctor, what does an anesthesiologist do." He always answers the question with the statement "We poison people." His statement is true. He deals in very skillfully controlled administration of doses of toxic chemicals that have the potential to be deadly.

We are familiar with household products and have learned to cope with their toxicological risks. It is when people are involuntarily exposed to toxins that the legal system becomes involved. Toxic substances are being deployed in tremendous quantities all through our environment every day without our knowledge or consent. Everyone is exposed to toxic substances daily in unknown dosages and in unknown mixtures. The combined health effects of most of the mixtures have never been studied. Chemicals are often used by people that have little knowledge or training concerning their harmful effects. My anesthesiologist friend once commented during direct examination that "I spent twelve years in college, medical school, internship, and residency learning to use my poisons. However, this pesticide applicator received one week's training, of which one day was watching video tapes and four days working with another applicator, after which he was turned loose to douse people's homes with multiple poisons."

With today's burgeoning proliferation of toxic chemicals broadcast by people knowing and caring little of the harm that they may cause, it is inevitable that injuries will occur. Government agencies are supposed to protect people from the untoward effects of exposure to toxic substances; however, they are often lax in fulfilling their responsibility. Consequently, it often falls to the tort law system to compensate victims who should never have been victims and to maintain the potential for litigation as a deterrent to rampant misuse of toxic chemicals.

To help deter the poisoning of America, the tort lawyer must be an effective advocate for his or her client. Litigation of a toxic tort case is not a skill that is taught in law schools. The attorney must learn the art and science of toxic tort litigation while in practice. The attorney may not even recognize a toxic tort case when one comes in the door. With this book the attorney will learn to recognize a toxic tort case and will know what to do with it.

The book is not intended to be an exhaustive tome with all the answers to every question. That would require an extensive library. It is intended to lay out the basic issues and concerns in a toxic tort case. It enables the practitioner to know a toxic tort case when it appears, how to set it up, organize it, determine the parties liable and understand enough about the chemicals involved in order to communicate knowledgeably about them. It will enable the advocate to appreciate the skills of the experts and allow the advocate to effectively communicate with experts and find ammunition for cross-examination.

Ernest P. Chiodo, J.D., M.D., M.P.H., M.S., M.B.A., C.I.H., is the ideal author for a work such as this. He is a physician board-certified in internal medicine and in occupational and environmental medicine. He is also one of the few physicians in the country who is also a Certified Industrial Hygienist. He has a Master of Public Health degree from Harvard University. He is not just an academic; he actively practices medicine. He also has a Juris Doctor degree that is not just for show. Attorney Chiodo has engaged in the actual conduct of jury trials. I know, since he has been my co-consul in several toxic tort cases in a number of jurisdictions. I have seen him argue motions, do jury selection, make opening statements, examine and cross-examine witnesses, and do closing arguments. He has done the full gamut of trial practice from initial client interviews through final judgment. He is an excellent trial lawyer, and I am not the only one who thinks so. I am glad when he is on my side. He also has testified as an expert medical witness many times. He knows every facet of toxic tort litigation from every aspect.

Dr. Chiodo provides within this book gems of researched law and accepted science polished with the grit of practical courtroom experience. If you do any toxic tort litigation, this book will soon become dog-eared and full of underlined passages. You will always keep it near.

Donnelly Wright Hadden, J.D.   Ann Arbor, Michigan

INTRODUCTION

This is a practical guide to assist the legal practitioner involved in toxic tort litigation. This book is written to give a brief overview of medical as well as legal topics that are important in toxic tort litigation. The author attempts to share the perspective of one that has been involved for a number of years in the field as a public health official, a medical practitioner, an expert witness, and as a trial attorney. The laws of the State of Michigan receive a special focus since Michigan is one of the most heavily industrialized areas in the world. As home of the "Arsenal of Democracy," Michigan has its fair share of toxin exposure cases. However, this book should be of assistance to legal practitioners outside of the State of Michigan. This is because the legal concepts that apply in Michigan may also apply in other jurisdictions. The additions by Daniel Breen and Mark Rouleau have added an Illinois flavor to the book. The fact that this book is used as the text book for the toxic tort law courses taught at John Marshall and Loyola University Law Schools in Chicago adds to this flavor. In addition, the scientific chapters cover concepts that have universal application without limitation by the borders of legal jurisdiction. It is written to be a guide for both the plaintiff and defense attorney in the practice of this difficult area of law. While the main audience for this book is likely to be attorneys, it may be of interest to law students and other professionals such as physicians, nurses, and industrial hygienists. While the underlying topic may be very difficult and technical, this book is meant to be light reading in conversational format. It is geared to be a "kitchen table" chat about the nuts and bolts of the practice of toxic tort litigation. It is not an extensive everything-you-need-to-know text. However, this book may provide some unique insights that are not likely to be available elsewhere.

This book is arranged in short chapters. While this is a book geared towards attorneys, not all the chapters mention law. Many chapters focus upon technical issues that are written at a level that can be understood by persons without prior technical expertise. These chapters are essential since the optimal practice of toxic tort law requires knowledge of the technical areas mentioned in this book.

PART ONE

LEGAL CONSIDERATIONS

WARNING

The first part of this book deals with some legal issues of particular importance in toxic tort litigation. The reader is warned to read this section with a mind open to the formation of his own professional opinion as to the merit of the various views and theories proposed. The reader is also warned that this section is only meant to serve as a starting point for the legal research that all readers should conduct prior to utilizing this information in their practice. This research should include a careful reading of all cases listed, as well as, a search for any contrary opinions. A diligent search for any change in the law can help avoid serious embarrassment and potential disaster.

CHAPTER ONE

WHAT IS TOXIC TORT LAW?

If the law is upheld only by government officials,
then all law is at an end.

Herbert Hoover
Message to Congress 1929

Toxic tort law is a specialized division of tort law. The main difference between a toxic tort case and other tort cases is that most torts deal with obvious physical injuries like a mutilated arm or a punch in the nose. These are the injuries that our legal forefathers were familiar with in medieval England. They were not familiar with cellular and sub-cellular damage arising from exposure to hazardous substances. Consequently, tort law did not fully develop over the centuries to address these injuries. The law is only now slowly adapting to properly address the issues involved in toxic tort cases.

The concept of damages arising from increased risk of disease due to a toxic exposure is fundamental to the understanding of toxic tort actions. It will frequently occur that a person, due to the negligence of another, is exposed to a toxic chemical and that the exposure places the person at a significantly increased risk of disease. However, that person is not currently suffering from any manifestation of disease due to the toxic exposure. They have no symptoms and lack any physical or laboratory findings to suggest current disease due to the toxic exposure. At first glance it may appear that there is liability but no damages. However, based upon epidemiological evidence, the exposed person may be at increased risk of disease. As a result they may recover damages arising out of this increased risk of disease (See Chapter Six: "Damages in Toxic Tort Litigation").

Another unique difficulty in toxic tort cases is establishment of causation. The scenario is frequently the following: A person is exposed to benzene due to the negligence of another. It is well known in the scientific literature that benzene causes leukemia. After an appropriate latency period, the exposed person develops leukemia.

Was the leukemia caused by the toxic exposure to benzene? The fate of the case will depend upon the answer to this question (See Chapter Five: "Causation in Toxic Tort Litigation").

Finally, few tort cases depend so heavy upon expert scientific testimony as will a toxic tort action. Issues concerning admissibility of expert scientific testimony and Daubert styled challenges are central to toxic tort litigation (See Chapter Three: "Expert Witnesses in Toxic Tort Litigation" and Chapter Four: "Daubert Rules Limiting Expert Witness Testimony").

Consequently, toxic tort actions differ from most other tort actions in the focus upon damages arising from increased risk, and difficulties concerning establishment of causation. In addition, toxic tort actions require extensive use of expert testimony with frequent Daubert styled challenges to admissibility of expert testimony.

CHAPTER TWO

PRACTICAL CONSIDERATIONS IN TOXIC TORT LAW

He that goes to law holds a wolf by the ears.

Robert Burton
Anatomy of Melancholy

Toxic tort law has some very interesting statistics associated with it. Of all the tort cases filed in state courts of general jurisdiction in the United States in 1992, approximately 2.7 percent went to a jury verdict. However, of the toxic tort cases filed, 6.5 percent went to a jury verdict. In toxic tort cases, the jury finds for the plaintiff 73 percent of the time. By comparison, the jury only finds for the plaintiff in 30 percent of trials concerning medical malpractice, and only 50 percent of the trials involving other professional malpractice including legal malpractice. In 1992, the median jury verdict in a toxic tort case was $101,000 and the mean was $530,000. The median jury award in a medical malpractice case was $201,000 and the mean was $1,057,000. *(Thomas H. Blaske. The New World Of Michigan Tort Reform: Survival Strategies. January 30, 1997. Troy, Michigan. Institute of Continuing Legal Education)*

The median is a statistical term referring to the value where half of the amounts are below the median and half are above the median. In the case of toxic tort jury awards, half of these jury awards were for less than $101,000; and half of the jury awards were for more than $101,000. The mean is the arithmetic average. Inordinately large or small awards can distort the mean. The large difference between the median and mean jury awards in toxic tort actions indicates that most jury awards were in the area of $100,000; but there were some tremendously large awards that distorted the average upward. It should also be noted that these are national figures that include some states allowing punitive damages. It is interesting that in 2001, the second largest jury verdict in the United States was $1 billion dollars in an environmental contamination case in Louisiana. *(Lawyers Weekly USA. January 7, 2002)*

What can be concluded from the above statistics? First, a toxic tort action is much more likely to go to trial than other tort cases. Second, if the case is tried, a jury is very likely to find for the plaintiff with a moderate award but not an unusually large award. However, large jury verdicts do occur, particularly in mass toxic tort cases.

The factors that influence the statistics behind toxic tort cases are interesting. The reason why a large percentage of toxic tort cases go to trial may be that the expert testimony that is required to establish the plaintiff's case in chief is difficult to obtain. There are a relatively small number of qualified medical experts available to provide expert testimony in toxic tort cases. As a result of limited supply and great demand, the time of a qualified medical expert in a toxic tort case is expensive. As a result, many toxic tort cases are filed without the availability of appropriate expert testimony in hopes of settlement. The insurance industry and the defense bar know this; consequently, settlements do not occur readily in this area of law. The defense is much more likely to put the plaintiff's case to the acid test by going to trial. However, if the plaintiff does put together the necessary elements of the case, and makes the required expenditures to obtain the time of an expert to testify; then a jury will frequently find in the plaintiff's favor. This jury propensity to find for the plaintiff in toxic tort cases coupled with the possibility of a sizable plaintiff award, often results in a settlement offer after the defense has been convinced that the plaintiff has credible expert testimony to make his case.

An important practical consideration for the plaintiff attorney is to beware of filing a toxic tort action if the attorney is not prepared to make necessary expenditures. These expenditures include time and funds in order to obtain the expert testimony necessary to establish the case. An approach based upon filing without the appropriate work-up of the case, with an eye towards an early settlement, is likely to meet with failure. The defense attorney should focus his or her attention upon seeking dismissal if the plaintiff has not obtained qualified experts to support his case.

CHAPTER THREE

A PRIMER ON TOXIC TORT LAW

By Mark Rouleau ©

Investigate Your Case Thoroughly

For which of you, intending to build a tower, does not first sit down and estimate the cost, to see whether he has enough to complete it? Luke 14:28

Facts

1. Damages—Most important issue from the beginning to end. No matter how good the liability if the damages are not big enough the case will be a flop. Judges & Juries will be more likely to find liability where the damages justify bringing the suit.

   a. Medical Records

      i. Billing Records
      ii. Lab reports
      iii. E1pidemiological testing by CDC and State agencies

   a. Employment Records
   b. Income Tax Filings
   c. Appearance of the plaintiff and his/her family. How will a jury connect with them and their plight?
   d. Alterations to Activities of daily living (ADL). The tasks of everyday life. Basic ADLs include eating, dressing, getting into or out of a bed or chair, taking a bath or shower, and using the toilet. Instrumental activities of daily living (IADL) are activities related to independent living and

include preparing meals, managing money, shopping, doing housework, and using a telephone. Also called activities of daily living.

2. Chemicals Involved—Get as much scientific literature, chemical, medical, toxicological and epidemiological as possible on the presumed or known bad actors. TOXNET and PubMed are a good places to start. If you can not find solid medical, and toxicological or epidemiological information showing known hazards with the specific chemicals involved you will have a very tough case and may not make it past summary judgment in federal court.

3. Defendant—Do an extensive investigation of the defendant. You need to know if they are likely to have coverage or financial ability to fund the damages. If you are dealing with a RCRA TSDF (Transfer Storage and Disposal Facility) there will be a wealth of public information available online).

  a. Web Search—review all of the documents you can find on the defendant, the chemicals and the technology. I suggest Googling every set of numbers of letters that you do not know or understand.

    i. SEC Filings—carefully review as these may indicate other suits and relevant facts or information. Monitor these sites as your case progresses to see if your case is reported to the shareholders and the public.
    ii. Defendant's Websites including past versions (see Internet Archive *http://www.archive.org/index.php* for archived versions of the web site). Often times you can make hay out of the changes either showing past claims or knowledge. You also need to inspect shadow sites.
    iii. Satellite Images—see Google Teraserver etc
    iv. Real Estate Records—for ownership and other possible defendants.
    v. Corporate Filings—Secretary of State records for officers and states of incorporation.
    vi. Dunn & Bradstreet—financial condition of the corporation.
    vii. Other Suits—Check Pacer and do a nationwide search on the defendant to look for other cases and other plaintiff attorneys who have sued the defendant. You can find pleadings online and you can contact the other attorneys to share information and discovery. Check the local court records in the County where the defendant

resides and/or does business as well as the location from which the liability arises.

    viii. State & Federal Regulatory Agencies i.e., the Illinois Environmental Protection Agency (IEPA), the Environmental Protection Agency (EPA), RCRA online, the Illinois Pollution Control Board (Note they have a text searchable database of cases and pleadings for enforcement actions online)

    ix. American Association for Justice (AAJ)—litigation exchange and work groups.

    x. State TLA

    xi. TrialSmith *www.trialsmith.com* for depositions, pleadings and other pending cases against the defendant

  b. Site Inspection—physically inspect the location and facilities involved. Bring a third party and take photos & measurements where possible. Having an Industrial Hygienist as the third person could be helpful at this point to identify possible problems.

  c. Freedom of Information (FOIA) Requests—send FOIA requests to the State and Federal Regulatory Agencies. This will not excuse issuing subpoenas to them later after suit is filed seeking the same information for many reasons including establishing presumptive admissibility as a public record.

  d. Common Law Petition for Discovery—if you are unaware of the specific facts necessary to evaluate a case (see for example Illinois Supreme Court Rule 224). The equitable bill of discovery was used to enable a plaintiff to obtain information and prepare his case for trial on the ultimate issues. (37 ALR 5th 645 (1996); 16 Ill.L. & Prac. Discovery § 2 (1971); *Poulos v. Parker Sweeper Co.*, 44 Ohio St. 3d 124, 541 N.E. 2d 1031 (Ohio, 1989); See, e.g., *Arcell v. Ashland Chemical Company, Inc.*, 152 N.J. Super. 471, 505-508, 378 A. 2d 53, 70-71 (1977); *Ross Stores, Inc. v. Redken Laboratories, Inc.*, 810 S.W. 2d 741 (Tex., 1991); *Sunbeam Television Corp. v. Columbia Broadcasting Sys.*, Inc., 694 F. Supp. 889, 891-92 (S.D. Fla. 1988).

4. Witness—talk with doctors if possible regarding possibility of chemical causation. You want to soften them up to the idea that there may have been a cause that they were not aware of if they did not make that initial diagnosis. You also need to explain to doctors the concept of "reasonable degree of

certainty" as it is a legal term of art unknown to most clinical physicians. Fellow employees, and former employees of the defendant can be crucial witnesses and may have very important knowledge. Other persons who may have been subjected to the toxic exposure. Talking with governmental enforcement personnel regarding inspections etc. is of great significance.

5. Causation—must be shown both medically and from an exposure basis. The standard for admissibility of expert testimony is therefore extremely important. Under Frey the admissibility of the expert opinions is nearly pro forma as long as it can be shown that the methodology employed (not the conclusions) are generally accepted in the relevant scientific community. Daubert on the other hand forces the judge to be an active participant weighing the credibility of the testimony and evidence. Thus in Daubert jurisdictions the motions to exclude testimony or the motion for summary judgment take on far greater significance.

    a. Federal & Daubert Jurisdictions—Basic Test 1) whether the expert's reasoning or methodology properly can be applied to the facts in issue; 2) whether the theory has been subjected to peer review or publications; and 3) the degree of acceptance within the relevant scientific community. A liability expert is only helpful to the fact finder if he is able to establish such an element of the claim through visual inspection, independent research, testing, and knowledge. *Clark v. Takata Corp., Am. Honda Motor*, 192 F. 3d 750 (7th Cir., 1999). An expert is to not required to have direct evidence or a personal observation of the cause of a VOC (volatile organic compound) pollution to provide opinions at to the cause of the pollution, as his opinion can be based on an inference embracing the ultimate issue. *NutraSweet Co. v. X-L Engineering Co.*, 227 F. 3d 776, 787-88 (7th Cir. 2000). Differential diagnosis is a common scientific technique, and federal courts, generally speaking, have recognized that a properly conducted differential diagnosis for causation is admissible under *Daubert*. See, e.g., *Westberry v. Gislaved Gummi AB*, 178 F. 3d 257 at 262-66 (4th Cir. 1999); *Heller v. Shaw Indus., Inc.*, 167 F. 3d 146, 154-55 (3d Cir. 1999); *Baker v. Dalkon Shield Claimants Trust*, 156 F. 3d 248, 252-53 (1st Cir. 1998); *Zuchowicz v. United States*, 140 F. 3d 381, 387 (2d Cir. 1998); *Ambrosini v. Labarraque*, 101 F. 3d 129, 140-41 (D.C. Cir. 1996); *Kennedy v. Collagen Corp.*, 161 F. 3d 1226 (9th Cir. 1998). "Thus, in evaluating the reliability of an opinion based on a differential diagnosis, courts look at the substance of the expert's analysis, rather than just the label. *See, e.g., Clausen,* 339 F. 3d at 1057-58 (advising courts to evaluate whether an expert, in conducting a differential diagnosis, has: (1) insured that the potential cause can in fact cause the injury; (2) taken care to consider other hypotheses that might otherwise explain a plaintiff's condition; and (3) taken care to explain why "the proffered alternative cause was ruled out."); *see also Heller v. Shaw Indus., Inc.,* 167 F. 3d 146, 155 (3d Cir. 1999) (explaining that the differential diagnosis method "'consists of a testable hypothesis,' has been peer reviewed, contains standards for controlling its operation, is generally accepted, and is used outside of the judicial context.") (citing *In re Paoli R.R. Yard PCB Litig.,* 35 F. 3d 717, 742 n. 8 (3d Cir. 1994))." *Bowers v. Norfolk Southern Corp., 537 F. Supp. 2d 1343* (M.D. Ga., 2007).

Some circuits have allowed clinical medical experts to testify to an opinion on causation as long as it is based on methods reasonably relied on by experts in their field. See, e.g., *Zuchowicz v. United States,* 140 F. 3d 381, 387 (2d Cir. 1998) (accepting the district court's conclusion that plaintiff's experts based their opinions on such methods). *Kennedy v. Collagen Corp.,* 161 F. 3d 1226 at 1230 (C.A. 9 (Cal.), 1998); *Hopkins v. Dow Corning Corp.,* 33 F. 3d 1116, 1125 (9th Cir. 1994) (finding admissible expert testimony of a rheumatologist based on medical records, his clinical experience, preliminary results of an epidemiological study and medical literature). Expert testimony is admissible absent epidemiological data in formulating their opinions *Kennedy v. Collagen Corp,* 161 F. 3d 1226 (9th Cir. 1998); *Benedi v. McNeil-P.P.C., Inc.,* 66 F. 3d 1378 (4th Cir. 1995).

The fact that a cause-effect relationship between substance and a particular disease has not been conclusively established does not render a physician's expert testimony on causation inadmissible. *Kennedy v. Collagen Corp.,* 161 F. 3d 1226 (C.A. 9 (Cal.), 1998) *Ambrosini v. Labarraque,* 101 F. 3d 129, 139 (D.C. Cir. 1996), cert. dismissed, *Upjohn Co. v. Ambrosini,*—U.S.—, 117 S. Ct. 1572, 137 L. Ed. 2d 716 (1997) (reversing district court's finding that expert testimony was inadmissible because none of the studies relied upon specifically concluded that Depo-Provera caused the type of birth defects suffered by the plaintiff). See also *Smolowitz v. Sherwin-Williams Co.,* 02-CV-5940 (CBA), 2008 U.S. Dist. LEXIS 91019, at *12-13 (E.D.N.Y. Nov. 10, 2008), 2008 WL 4862981 (noting in toxic tort case involving paint product chemicals that some cases suggest "that treating physicians may render expert opinion testimony regarding causation even without submitting a detailed report" however the opinion must quantify the amount of the substance the plaintiff was exposed to (dosing) and that the amount of toxin the person was exposed to is capable of causing the disease.

A plaintiff does not need to produce a mathematically precise table equating levels of exposure with levels of harm in order to show that they were exposed to a toxic level of a substance but only 'evidence from which a reasonable person could conclude' that the exposure probably caused plaintiff's injuries. *Bonner v. ISP Technologies Inc.*, 259 F. 3d 924 (8th Cir., 2001). In many toxic tort cases it is impossible to quantify exposure with hard proof, such as the presence of the alleged toxic substance in the plaintiff's blood or tissue and the exact amount of the toxic substance to which an individual plaintiff was exposed therefore, expert opinions regarding toxic injuries is admissible where dosage or exposure levels have been demonstrated through sufficiently reliable circumstantial evidence. *Plourde v. Gladstone*, 190 F. Supp. 2d 708, 721 (D. Vt. 2002). Even if a judge believes there are better grounds for some alternative conclusion, and that there are flaws in the scientist's methods, if there are good grounds for the expert's conclusion, it should be admitted. The district court cannot exclude scientific testimony simply because the conclusion was 'novel' if the methodology and the application of the methodology are reliable. *Bonner v. ISP Technologies Inc.*, 259 F. 3d 924.

In *Goebel v. Denver and Rio Grande Western R. Co.*, 346 F. 3d 987 (10th Cir., 2003) the court held there is no requirement that each individual article must fully support the expert's precise theory noting that studies may support a conclusion either "individually *or in combination.*" (346 F. 3d 987, 993).

In order to qualify for admission, expert's opinion as to causation need not eliminate all other potential causes; expert's opinion as to probable cause admissible so long as it is based on facts and sound methodology. *Mihailovich v. Laatsch*, 359 F. 3d 892 (7th Cir., 2004).

For purposes of admissibility under *Daubert* purposes, temporal and geographic proximity with toxic releases and the onset of a disease is a sufficient scientific basis for considering the toxic release as a possible cause of the disease. *Clausen v. M/V New Carissa*, 339 F. 3d 1049 at 1059 (9th Cir., 2003). The fact that the minimum threshold level of toxins necessary to cause harm has not yet been established with any degree of certainty does not render an expert's opinions mere guesswork. *Clausen*, 339 F. 3d 1049 at 1059. A lack of specific scholarly support does not prevent the admission of *differential diagnosis* testimony: "The fact that a cause-effect relationship . . . has not been conclusively established does not render [the expert's] testimony inadmissible." *Clausen*, 339 F. 3d 1049 at 1059; see also *Kennedy v. Collagen Corp.*, 161 F. 3d 1226 (9th Cir. 1998). The case law specific to *differential diagnosis* recognizes that the absence of peer-reviewed studies does not in itself prevent an expert from ruling in a diagnostic hypothesis that might explain the patient's symptoms. *Clausen*, 339 F. 3d 1049 at 1060. *Bonner v. ISP Technologies Inc.*, 259 F. 3d 924 (8th Cir., 2001).

The fact that a cause-effect relationship between substance and a particular disease has not been conclusively established does not render a physician's expert testimony on causation inadmissible. *Kennedy v. Collagen Corp.*, 161 F. 3d 1226 (C.A. 9 (Cal.), 1998) *Ambrosini v. Labarraque*, 101 F. 3d 129, 139 (D.C. Cir. 1996), cert. dismissed, *Upjohn Co. v. Ambrosini,*—U.S.—, 117 S. Ct. 1572, 137 L. Ed. 2d 716 (1997)(reversing district court's finding that expert testimony was inadmissible because none of the studies relied upon specifically concluded that Depo-Provera caused the type of birth defects suffered by the plaintiff).

i.   General Causation (Scientific Possibility)—Scientific information medical, toxicological or epidemiological establishing the relationship between a bad actor that was present and the type of injury, damage or disease that occurred;

ii. Proximity & Possible Dosing—Toxicological and/or Industrial Hygienic—actual presence of the toxic substance in sufficient quantities to cause the harm, injury or damage complained of.

iii. Medical Causation—toxic substance more likely than not caused (to a reasonable degree of medical or scientific certainty) that harm, injury or damage complained of.

A court must be careful not to cross the boundary between gatekeeper and trier of fact. *Milward v. Acuity Specialty Prod.s Group Inc* (1st Cir., 2011). "The soundness of the factual underpinnings of the expert's analysis and the correctness of the expert's conclusions based on that analysis are factual matters to be determined by the trier of fact." *Smith v. Ford Motor Co*, 215 F. 3d 713 at 718, 721 (7th Cir. 2000). "When the factual underpinning of an expert's opinion is weak, it is a matter affecting the weight and credibility of the testimony—a question to be resolved by the jury." *United States v. Vargas*, 471 F. 3d 255 at 264, 265 (1st Cir. 2006) 471 F. 3d at 264 (quoting *Int'l Adhesive Coating Co. v. Bolton Emerson Int'l*, 851 F. 2d 540, 545 (1st Cir. 1988)); see also *Quiet Tech. DC-8, Inc. v. Hurel-Dubois UK Ltd.*, 326 F. 3d 1333, 1345 (11th Cir. 2003); *Amorgianos v. Nat'l R.R. Passenger Corp.*, 303 F. 3d 256, 267 (2d Cir. 2002).

b. Illinois & Frye Jurisdictions—In a significant minority of jurisdictions[1] including Illinois to guarantee the reliability of new or novel scientific evidence. "Illinois, the exclusive test for the admission of expert testimony is governed by the standard first expressed in *Frye v. United States*, 293 F. 1013 (D.C. Cir. 1923). *Donaldson v. Central Illinois Public Service Co.*, 199 Ill. 2d 63, 262 Ill. Dec. 854, 767 N.E. 2d 314 (2002)" See *People v. McKown*, (Ill. 2007) 2007 WL 2729262, 226 Ill. 2d 245.

"Commonly called the "general acceptance" test, the *Frye* standard dictates that scientific evidence is admissible at trial only if the methodology or scientific principle upon which the opinion is based is "sufficiently established to have gained general acceptance in the particular field in which it belongs." *Frye*, 293 F. at 1014. In this context, "general acceptance" does not mean universal acceptance, and it does not require that the methodology in question be accepted by unanimity, consensus, or even a majority of experts. *Donaldson*, 199 Ill. 2d at 78, 262 Ill. Dec. 854, 767 N.E. 2d 314. Instead, evidence meets the *Frye* standard if the underlying method used to generate an expert's opinion is reasonably relied upon by experts in the relevant field. *Donaldson*, 199 Ill. 2d at 77, 262 Ill. Dec. 854, 767 N.E. 2d 314. Significantly, the *Frye* test applies only to "new" or "novel" scientific methodologies. *Donaldson*, 199 Ill. 2d at 78-79, 262 Ill. Dec. 854, 767 N.E. 2d 314. Generally, a scientific methodology is considered "new" or "novel" if it is "'original or striking'" or "does 'not resembl[e] something formerly known or used.'" *Donaldson*, 199 Ill. 2d at 79, 262 Ill. Dec. 854, 767 N.E. 2d 314, quoting Webster's

---

[1]   Alabama, Arizona, California, Florida, Illinois, Kansas, Maryland, Minnesota, New Jersey, New York, Pennsylvania, and Washington.

Third New International Dictionary 1546 (1993)." *Northern Trust Co. v. Burandt and Armbrust, LLP*, (Ill. App. 2 Dist. 2010) 933 N.E. 2d 432 at 445, 403 Ill. App. 3d 260.

The Frye test *does not* make the trial judge a "gatekeeper" of all expert opinion testimony; the trial judge applies the Frye test only if the scientific principle, technique or test offered by the expert to support his or her conclusion is "new" or "novel." (*Donaldson* 767 N.E. 2d 314, at 324-25). The Illinois Supreme Court in *Donaldson* stated in some cases "medical science does not seek to establish the existence of a cause and effect relationship—for example, in this instance, the small number of neuroblastoma cases limits study of the disease. As a result, extrapolation offers those with rare diseases the opportunity to seek a remedy for the wrong they have suffered. Thus, in these limited instances, an expert may rely upon scientific literature discussing similar, yet not identical, cause and effect relationships. The fact that an expert must extrapolate, and is unable to produce specific studies that show the exact cause and effect relationship to support his conclusion, affects the weight of the testimony rather than its admissibility. * * * In a courtroom, the test for allowing a plaintiff to recover in a tort suit of this type is not scientific certainty but legal sufficiency; if reasonable jurors could conclude from the expert testimony that [the chemical] more likely than not caused [plaintiff's] injury, the fact that another jury might reach the opposite conclusion or that science would require more evidence before conclusively considering the causation question resolved is irrelevant." (767 N.E. 2d 328-329).

c. Standard of Proof—Reasonable degree of Medical or Scientific Certainty:

Research has indicated that "reasonable medical certainty" is a concept unheard of in the day-to-day practice of medicine. Several authors have indicated that the legal profession to allow for the introducing testimony involving medical judgment created the expression. It seems that the phrase has its origins in Illinois case law beginning in the 1930's and became widely used throughout the nation as a result of a popular trial technique book of the day. (*Goldstein's Trial Technique*, 1935 ed; Jeff L. Lewin, *The Genesis and Evolution of Legal Uncertainty About "Reasonable Medical Certainty*,*"* 57 Maryland L. Rev. 380, 381 (1998).)

"In the case of expert medical testimony, we are accustomed to a doctor's opinion being prefaced by the phrase "within a reasonable degree of medical certainty." This phrase gives the medical opinion its legal perspective. It allows us to know that the opinion is an expression of medical probability based upon recognized medical thought and not mere guess or speculation. (See *Boose v. Digate* (1969), 107 Ill. App. 2d 418, 246 N.E. 2d 50.) But, there is no magic to the phrase itself. If the testimony of the expert reveals that his or her opinions are based upon specialized knowledge and experience and grounded in recognized medical thought, it is of no consequence that the witness has failed to preface the opinions with the phrase, "within a reasonable degree of medical certainty." See *Redmon v. Sooter* (1971), 1 Ill. App. 3d 406, 412, 274 N.E. 2d 200; Boose, 107 Ill. App. 2d at 422-24, 246 N.E. 2d 50." *Dominguez v. St. John's Hosp.*, (Ill. App. 1 Dist. 1993) 632 N.E. 2d 16 at 19, 260 Ill. App. 3d 591.

Black's Law Dictionary defines "reasonable medical probability" as "a standard requiring a showing that the injury was *more likely than not* caused by a particular stimulus, based on the general consensus of recognized medical thought." Black's Law Dictionary 1273 (8th ed. 2004). Black's treats the term "reasonable medical certainty" as a synonym of "reasonable medical probability." Thus, Black's seems to subscribe to the view that "reasonable degree of medical certainty" simply means that, based upon generally accepted medical principles, the statement is more likely than not to be true. The definition as stated in Black's Law Dictionary is not universally accepted.

The Law

6.   Theories of Liability—the "Rules of the Road" approach Create an initial set of jury instructions from the very outset. These are the standards by which your case will be judged. It cannot be over stressed just how important this step is. Most attorneys do not start their draft jury instructions until shortly before a trial. This is a serious error.

"The defense wields three weapons to defeat plaintiffs' cases that should be won:

- Complexity,
- Confusion, and

- Ambiguity.

Complexity, confusion and *ambiguity* are insidious enemies. They creep up when you are not looking. They rarely attack head-on. They are particularly abundant and pernicious in complex cases such as *[toxic torts,]* insurance bad faith or medical malpractice. This is because both the facts and the jury instructions in these cases are often complex, confusing and ambiguous. But these enemies appear in simple cases too.

Sometimes, *complexity, confusion* and *ambiguity* are inherent in the case; other times, they proliferate due to a conscious defense strategy of confounding the jury and judge with endless, immaterial detail. In either event, you must defeat complexity, confusion and ambiguity, or they will defeat you." RULES OF THE ROAD: A Plaintiff's Lawyers Guide to Proving Liability, Rick Friedman.

Jury instructions are loaded with the terms like "reasonable" and "negligent" which have little or no *real meaning* to jurors outside of every day activities with which they are personally familiar and in complex cases such as toxic torts are likely to be areas for the defense to exploit confusion on the part of the jurors to relieve their clients from responsibility for their acts. Toxic tort cases are not like simple auto cases where most members of the jury know what the "rules of the road" are and they know when someone violated them. In auto cases jurors generally don't need to be provided with special guidance for determining fault and negligence or reasonableness of the defendant's conduct. However, in toxic tort cases jurors have no real idea regarding the reasonableness of the defendants conduct with respect to the handling, warning, storage (ect.) of the toxic substances. The defendant will exploit any complexity, confusion or ambiguity that exists in this area causing an otherwise good case to be lost. You need to fill the vague concepts of "negligence" and "reasonable" or "reasonableness" with meaning in simple straightforward terms that the jury can use to measure the defendant's conduct.

You need to establish basic standards of conduct that the defendant failed to comply with. In creating this "rules of the road" list you will need to keep four (4) criteria in mind when creating your rules list: (1) the rule must be easily understood and expressed (i.e. Warning labels are required on containers containing more than 0.05% XYZ); (2) it must be on a point that you believe the defense will concede or that you can otherwise easily prove in the absence of the defendant's agreement; (3) it must have been violated by the defendant; and (4) it is serious and material enough that a jury would decide the case in your favor based upon its violation.

Create a list of your theories of liability (rules list) which you will constantly annotate with references (with evidentiary materials sources showing both to breaches of the rule the sources for the rules) and to which you will add rules as you proceed with your case. This working list of the rules when finalized for trial will be the skeleton for your entire presentation with respect to liability. This will allow you to show both duty and breach by demonstrating the standard of conduct for the defendant as well as the breach of that standard. Some basic sources for locating rules for your lists are case law, statutes, codes, policy manuals, industry standards, scientific & medical literature, depositions, etc. Proper preparation and annotation of your rules list will be of great assistance with preparing your pleadings, interrogatories, document requests, responses to motions seeking to limit discovery, motions for summary judgment and trial presentation.

Theories of liability upon which toxic torts may be premised:

a. Common Law

i. Premises—failure to warn of a dangerous condition or activity on the premises of which the owner has superior knowledge.

ii. Negligence—handling, warning, signage, transportation etc.

1. Breach of Internal Standards—"the failure of a clinic to follow its policies can be evidence of a breach of the clinic's duty to a patient." *Adams v. Family Planning Associates Medical Group, Inc.*, 315 Ill. App. 3d at 548, 248 Ill. Dec. 91, 733 N.E. 2d 766; *Smith v. Silver Cross Hosp.*, (Ill. App. 1 Dist. 2003) 790 N.E. 2d 77, 339 Ill. App. 3d 67.

2. Breach of Statutory or Regulatory Requirements—"A violation of a statute or ordinance designed to protect human life or property is prima facie evidence of negligence. (*Barthel v. Illinois Central Gulf R.R. Co.*, (1978) 74 Ill. 2d 213, 219.) A party injured by such a violation may recover only by showing that the violation proximately caused his injury and the statute or ordinance was intended to protect a class of persons to which he belongs from the kind of injury that he suffered. (*Barthel*, 74 Ill. 2d at 219-20 [23 Ill. Dec. 529, 384 N.E. 2d 323]; *Ney v. Yellow Cab Co.*, (1954) 2 Ill. 2d 74, 76-79.)" *Recio v. GR-MHA*

Corp., (Ill. App. 1 Dist. 2006) 851 N.E. 2d 106 at 115, 366 Ill. App. 3d 48.

    a.   Municipal Codes (Chemical storage codes frequently contained in local fire codes).

    b.   State Regulations

    c.   Federal Regulations (RCRA, CERCLA, OSHA etc.) (2000). In *Ross v. Dae Julie, Inc.*, 341 Ill. App. 3d 1065, 1074, 275 Ill. Dec. 588, 793 N.E. 2d 68 (2003), the court held that although a violation of OSHA regulations may be evidence of failure to exercise reasonable care, OSHA regulations do not create a duty of care. "OSHA does not create duties owed by employers to mere invitees upon the premises of employers." *Kerker v. Elbert*, 261 Ill. App. 3d at 928, 199 Ill. Dec. at 646, 634 N.E. 2d at 485; *Barrera v. E.I. Du Pont De Nemours & Co.* (5th Cir. 1981), 653 F. 2d 915, 920.

3.   Negligent labeling or warning (See *Wyeth v. Levine*, No. 06-1249 (U.S. 3/4/2009) (2009))

4.   Negligent performance of voluntary undertaking—Generally, pursuant to the voluntary undertaking theory of liability, "one who undertakes, gratuitously or for consideration, to render services to another is subject to liability for bodily harm caused to the other by one's failure to exercise due care in the performance of the undertaking." *Wakulich v. Mraz*, (Ill. 2003) 785 N.E. 2d 843 at 854, 203 Ill. 2d 223; *Rhodes v. Illinois Central Gulf R.R.*, 172 Ill. 2d 213, 239, 216 Ill. Dec. 703, 665 N.E. 2d 1260 (1996).

5.   Res Ipsa Loquitur—*Smith v. Illinois Cent. R.R. Co.*, (Ill. 2006) 860 N.E. 2d 332, 223 Ill. 2d 441; *Reynolds Metals Company v. Yturbide*, 258 F. 2d 321 (9th Cir., 1958); *Farm Services, Inc. v. Gonzales*, 756 S.W. 2d 747 (Tex. App.-Corpus Christi, 1988); *Gass v. Marriott Hotel Services, Inc.*, 558 F. 3d 419 (6th Cir., 2009).

iii.   Trespass—*Smith*, supra

iv. Civil Conspiracy—the combination or two or more persons or entities for the purpose of accomplishing by concerted action either an unlawful purpose or a lawful purpose by unlawful means. *Lewis v. Lead Industries Ass'n, Inc.*, (Ill. App. 1 Dist. 2003) 793 N.E. 2d 869, 342 Ill. App. 3d 95; *McClure v. Owens Corning Fiberglas Corp.*, 188 Ill. 2d 102, 133, 241 Ill. Dec. 787, 720 N.E. 2d 242 (1999).

v. Products—

1. Strict Liability

   a. Warning or Labeling. See, Wyeth v. Levine, No. 06-1249 (U.S. 3/4/2009) (2009) citing to *Bates* v. *Dow Agrosciences LLC,* 544 U. S. 431, 451 (2005) (noting that state tort suits "can serve as a catalyst" by aiding in the exposure of new dangers and prompting a manufacturer or the federal agency to decide that a revised label is required). See also, *Gray v. National Restoration Systems, Inc.*, (Ill. App. 1 Dist. 2004) 820 N.E. 2d 943, 354 Ill. App. 3d 345 (where plaintiff's estate sued manufacturer and distributor for improper labeling which exploded from sparks when decedent was fatally injured when he attempted to saw the lid off an emptied 55-gallon drum that contained residue of Chem-Trete BSM 20, consisting of 70% ethanol and 10% methanol.) See *Tyler Enterprises of Elwood, Inc. v. Skiver*, (Ill. App. 3 Dist. 1994) 633 N.E. 2d 1331, 260 Ill. App. 3d 742, (reversing trial court's grant of summary judgment to manufacturer on property damage suit brought in strict liability claim in products alleging that the MSDS and label on chemical drum was misleading). Products claims in strict liability have also been sustained for parts inspectors who suffered injuries as result of contact with rust preventative oil on parts shipped by a component manufacturer due to their failure to provide sufficient warnings. *Goldman v. Walco Tool & Engineering Co.*, (Ill. App. 1 Dist. 1993) 614 N.E. 2d 42, 243 Ill. App. 3d 981 (parts manufacturer received knowledge of danger of the rust preventative oil through drum labeling it received but failed to communicate it persons handling the parts that were to be incorporated into tractors).

i. Insecticide, Fungicide, and Rodenticide Labels. The Insecticide, Fungicide, and Rodenticide Act (FIFRA) (7 U.S.C. § 136v(b) (1994)) section 136v(b) expressly preempts only state-law claims that challenge the adequacy of the warnings or other information on a pesticide's approved product label which are in addition to or different from those required under [FIFRA]," §136v(b). *Bates v. Dow Agrosciences LLC,* 544 U.S. 431, 125 S. Ct. 1788, 161 L. Ed. 2d 687 (2005),

The Insecticide, Fungicide, and Rodenticide Act (FIFRA) does not preempt state law based causes of action premised upon defective design, defective manufacture, negligent testing, and breach of express warranty claims. *Bates v. Dow Agrosciences LLC,* 544 U.S. 431, 125 S. Ct. 1788, 161 L. Ed. 2d 687 (2005).

FIFRA does not provide a federal remedy to those injured as a result of a manufacturer's violation of FIFRA's labeling requirements, nothing in §136v(b) precludes States from providing such a remedy. *Bates v. Dow Agrosciences LLC,* 544 U.S. 431, 125 S. Ct. 1788, 161 L. Ed. 2d 687 (2005).

"Under FIFRA, a pesticide is "misbranded" if its labeling contains statements that are "false or misleading in any particular," the pesticide's labeling does not contain directions for use which are "necessary for effecting the purpose for which the product is intended," or "the label does not contain a warning or caution statement which may be necessary . . . to protect health and the environment." 7 U.S.C. § 136(q)(1)." *Indian Brand Farms Inc v. Novartis Crop Prot. Inc,* 617 F. 3d 207 (3rd Cir., 2010). A product pamphlet does not constitute a label. *Indian Brand*

Farms Inc v. Novartis Crop Prot. Inc, 617 F. 3d 207 (3rd Cir., 2010).

FIFRA's misbranding provisions require "warning[s] or caution statement[s] which may be necessary . . . to protect health and the environment." 7 U.S.C. § 136(q)(1)(G). The "term 'environment' includes water, air, land, and all plants and man and other animals living therein . . . ." § 136(j); *Kuiper v. Am. Cyanamid*, 131 F. 3d 656, 664 (7th Cir. 1997); *Etcheverry v. Tri-Ag Serv., Inc.*, 22 Cal. 4th 316, 93 Cal. Rptr. 2d 36, 993 P. 2d 366, 375 (2000). *Indian Brand Farms Inc v. Novartis Crop Prot. Inc*, 617 F. 3d 207 (3rd Cir., 2010).

    b.   Negligent Manufacture—See for example *Stevenson v. Keene Corp.*, 603 A. 2d 521, 527-28 (N.J. Super. Ct. App. Div. 1992) recognizing that "exposure to asbestos caused by negligent manufacture, use, disposal, handling, storage and treatment with resulting injury is a 'tort against the environment,' . . . involving a hazardous and toxic substance")

    c.   Negligent Design—See for example In re Agent Orange" Product Liability Litigation, 517 F. 3d 76 (2nd Cir., 2008)

  vi. Warranty—labeling, instruction MSDS (Material Safety Data Sheet)

    1.   Express—See for example Thunander v. Uponor, Inc. (D. Minn., August 14, 2012) Civil No. 11-2322 (SRN/SER)

    2.   Implied

  vii. Material Misrepresentation

    1.   Intentional

    2.   Negligent

viii. Ultrahazardous or Inherently Dangerous Activity—"that the defendant will be liable when he damages another by a thing or activity unduly dangerous and inappropriate to the place where it is maintained, in the light of the character of that place and its surroundings." Prosser & Keeton on Torts Sec. 78, at 547-48 (W. Keeton 5th ed. 1984). See also The Restatement (Second) of Torts §§ 519-520 (1977). (1) storage of toxic gas, (*Langlois v. Allied Chemical Corp.*, 258 La. 1067, 249 So. 2d 133 (1971) (2) crop dusting with airplanes; *Roberts v. Cardinal Services Inc.*, 266 F. 3d 368 (5th Cir., 2001) citing to *Kent v. Gulf States Utilities*, 418 So. 2d 493, 498 (La. 1982); The court in *Luthringer v. Moore*, 31 Cal. 2d 489, 190 P. 2d 1 (1948), applied strict liability based on the ultrahazardous activity doctrine in connection with the use of hydrocyanic acid gas in fumigating a small shop to exterminate vermin. Storage of flammable liquids. *Kosters v. Seven-Up Co.*, 595 F. 2d 347, 354 (6th Cir. 1979). Disposal of by-product of chemical substances identified as dichlorobutadiene, containing heavy concentrations of organic chlorides. identified by the symbols BR50 and BR68, is an ultrahazardous activity because those substances are generally inimical to the environment: specifically, they are toxic and harmful to persons on touch or inhalation, corrosive to metals and other materials, noxiously malodorous, and pollutants of ground and surface water and plant and animal life. *Ashland Oil, Inc. v. Miller Oil Purchasing Co.*, 678 F. 2d 1293 (C.A. 5 (La.), 1982). See also EPA doc. 9477. 1993(01) (opinion letter dated October 4, 1993) entitled "Potential Liability Of Disposal Facilities When Disposing Of Contaminated Debris" "A rule of strict liability applies under RCRA, so that a disposal facility can be liable for improper disposal of untreated waste even if it does so in the good faith belief that the treatment standard does not apply." See also *Hazardous wastes strict liability : report to the 1985 General Assembly of North Carolina* (1984).[2] But see *Ganton Technologies, Inc. v. Quadion Corporation*, 834 F. Supp. 1018 (N.D. Ill., 1993) or *Indiana Harbor Belt R. Co. v. American Cyanamid Co.*, 916 F. 2d 1174 (7th Cir. 1990). *Fritz v. E.I. DuPont de Nemours & Co.*, 45 Del. 427, 75 A. 2d 256 (1950), rejected the ultrahazardous activity doctrine and held that

---

[2]   *http://www.archive.org/stream/hazardouswastess00nort#page/12/mode/2up*

business operator was not strictly liable as a result of the escape of harmful gases from his premises. storage of anhydrous ammonia at a chemical plant was not an ultrahazardous activity for purposes of imposing strict liability because the inherent odor characteristics of the chemical made it highly likely that people would recognize the escape of the chemical and be able to take safety precautions such as "moving away from the close proximity of the source of the gas once its odor is detected". *Sprankle v. Bower Ammonia & Chemical Co.*, 824 F. 2d 409 (C.A. 5 (Miss.), 1987)

ix. Nuisance—Toxic tort case involving neuroblastoma due to coal tar seeping into ground water. *Donaldson v. Central Illinois Public Service Co.*, (Ill. 2002) 767 N.E. 2d 314, 199 Ill. 2d 63. Whether smoke, odors, dust or gaseous fumes constitute a nuisance depends on the peculiar facts presented by each case." *City of Chicago v. Commonwealth Edison Co.*, 24 Ill. App. 3d 624, 631-32, 321 N.E. 2d 412 (1974).

b. Contract—undertakings with plaintiff or third party (where plaintiff is a third party beneficiary) establishing a contractual duty on the part of the defendant to warn or provide protection to the plaintiff.

c. Statutory—

i. Comprehensive Environmental Response, Compensation, and Liability Act (CERCLA)

ii. Resource Conservation and Recovery Act (RCRA)

iii. State Statutes and regulations

iv. Municipal Codes

v. State Regulations

vi. Federal Regulations

7. Admissibility of Evidence—what evidence will the jury hear. You must carefully examine and prepare memos for the foundations, exclusions, privileges etc. of all the significant evidence you intend to present in the case. Begin making motions in limine and responses to motions in limine as you continue to work on your case. Each time you encounter a significant piece of evidence ask yourself will it be admitted into evidence; and if you were the defendant how would you argue to keep it out? You must be able to examine the case from both the plaintiff and defendant's perspective in order to

successfully anticipate these types of challenges. Expect that every damaging piece of evidence no matter how clear will be challenged by the defense and you must be thoroughly prepared in advance for these challenges.

8. Jury Instructions—start working on your instructions from the very beginning of the case. They will be the law as given to the jury. As with the motions in limine create a sub-file folder with your research on these as they come up. You are bound to find material in the cases you encounter that will be the basis for later instruction to the jury.

Locating Experts

You need to determine the type of experts that you will need for your case. Most toxic tort cases will need:

1. Medical Causation Expert,
2. Toxicologist, Epidemiologist, Occupational Medicine Physician
3. Industrial Hygienist
4. Other experts regarding industry duties and standards of care
5. Damages Expert (physiatrist or life care planner),
6. Economist (to present value the future damages)

Once you have determined the experts that will be needed you should use many of the resources listed in the fact investigation area to locate experts. I recommend staying away from expert locater companies. State Trial Lawyer Association (TLA's) discussion groups are a good source for information on experts (both yours and your opponents). Westlaw has a fantastic expert witness research tool that allows you to find all opinions, and depositions that are filed by experts in federal cases and many state cases. TrialSmith has a very large deposition database of defense experts. Many of the State Jury Reporters maintain deposition databases as well. You will want witnesses who are credible and you shouldn't push a case forward if your liability and causation experts are hesitant or feel uncomfortable with the case. You will only waste your time and money on a case that will likely fail.

Theme the Case

You have to be able to explain your case in a simple paragraph in order to succeed with a jury. This is where your "rules of the road" list will be very helpful. By the time that complete discovery you should be able to reduce your rules list into a list of no more than twelve points. You will want to pare down the list to the clearest violations that best support your claim for damages.

Information overload: *"The Magical Number Seven, Plus or Minus Two: Some Limits on Our Capacity for Processing Information"* is a 1956 paper by the cognitive psychologist George A. Miller of Princeton University's Department of Psychology. In it Dr. Miller showed a number of remarkable coincidences between the channel capacity of a number of human cognitive and perceptual tasks. In each case, the effective channel capacity is equivalent to between 5 and 9 equally-weighted error-less choices: on average, about 2.5 bits of information. Make sure to use the KISS principle when theming your case Keep it Short & Simple ("Keep it Simple, Stupid"). Simplicity should be a key goal and that unnecessary complexity should be avoided. Rely upon ordinary prejudices and first impressions (they will rarely fail you when dealing with juries). Remember that we want to avoid the three traps of *complexity, confusion, and ambiguity*, in which many good plaintiff cases are lost. If you don't eliminate these traps by your rules you are sure to have the defendant argue that how could they have possibly forseen this problem or the consequences where it so complex, confusing and/or ambigious.

The theme of the case should be woven throughout all of your pleadings, discovery, pre-trial preparation of evidence and witnesses, exhibits, opening argument, evidence, closing arguments and concluded in the jury instructions. A simple coherent straightforward theme:

You are here to fix a wrong. This case is about choices. The defendant chose not to warn Mr._____ of the extremely dangerous witches brew of toxic chemicals present at the defendant's business. Choosing not to tell Mr. _____ the truth of that danger was just wrong. The defendant knew that XYZ was an extremely toxic chemical and that it was present everywhere at _____. Yet the defendant chose to tell Mr. _____ that he was handling "non-hazardous waste." The defendant requires its own employees to use respirators where chemical XYZ is present. The defendant chose not to require Mr. _____ to use respirators where chemical XYZ was present. Federal law required the defendant to warn its employees of the presence of chemical XYZ. The defendant chose not to warn Mr. _____ of the presence of chemical XYZ. Federal law and industry standards require the defendant to place a warning label on any containers containing the chemical XYZ. Although the containers delivered to Mr. _____ contained some chemical XYZ the defendant chose not to put a label the containers delivered to Mr. _____ .

The defendant chose not to give any warnings regarding the presence of chemical XYZ to (use plaintiff's first name). The defendant and its experts admit that chemical XYZ is scientifically documented to cause _____ . (Plaintiff's first name) suffered a permanent and irreversible brain injury as a result of exposure to that XYZ. He is now a paraplegic restricted to a wheelchair for the remainder of his life because of the choices of defendant _____ .

The theme should follow the "Rules of the Road" & "Ball on Damages" approach. That is there are minimum expectations for conduct in any given circumstance, and that the defendant chose not to follow those standards. We all live with rules for our mutual benefit. When someone breaks the rules or goes outside the rules others get hurt. Demonstrate that your client was harmed because the defendant chose not to follow the rules and failed to adhere to widely accepted standards of conduct in the defendant's industry. This approach embraces the conservative beliefs that there are rules of proper behavior, those rules must be followed, and anyone breaking those rules is responsible for the consequences.

"Your are going to learn from the evidence, the principles and standards for _____ and for this particular _____ .

These rules are just as basic and common to _____ as driving a car is to you. To understand what this case is about and how to understand to make the right decision in this case, you need to understand these basic rules or principles and standards. Now, I am going to show you what the defendant is going to agree to, what they admit are those basis rules and standards which they agree they have to abide by. (Then show the jury on a separate board, each of the standards, which the defendant is going to be judged upon, read each one aloud.)

You are going to hear evidence from _____ own _____ and _____ who will agree that these are the basic standards that they have to be held accountable for, and that they have this obligation to [Plaintiff]. You are going to hear evidence that every reputable _____ understands and agrees with these principles. Indeed you are going to hear evidence that the _____ and executives at [Defendant] agree that they should be accountable if these laws, regulations, policies standards and principles are violated.

During this trial, we will prove to you that these principles were violated by [Defendant] when they _____.

Theme the case from the beginning to show the rules and how they were broken. Remember when you present a case you know what you want and the defense knows what it wants, but you are placing your dispute before twelve members of our community to decide. They have their own needs and wants. What does the jury want and what do they get out of hearing these cases. If you don't give them what they need to help you win your case the defense will. The defense will convince them that all of the woes in the world, including the bad economy etc. are as a result of trials, and trial lawyers. You need to let the jury know from the beginning that they are given the very important responsibility of fixing wrongs. They can make the world a better place by fixing a wrong. Then you have to show them what the defendant did was wrong and it is best if you make the jury mad about the defendant's conduct that is why you should refer to their conduct as choices and not just as failures. For example the defendant took enough time to come up with a safety policy for their employees why didn't they do the same for workers coming on to their property. These kinds of differences should be highlighted where the defendant has instituted different policies in different jurisdictions and your situation involves the policy with the lower standards. Be creative but show the wrong, and explain why it is wrong. Repeat the wrong every chance you get.

CHAPTER FOUR

CAUSATION IN TOXIC TORT LITIGATION

And now remains that we find out the cause of this effect; Or rather say, the cause of this defect, for this effect defective comes by cause.

William Shakespeare
Hamlet II. ii.

That evil is half-cured whose cause we know.

Charles Churchill
Gotham III

The question of causation is central to toxic substances litigation. The point is well demonstrated in Jonathan Harr's book, *A Civil Action*. The case involved trichloroethylene (TCE) contamination of the municipal water supply in the City of Woburn, Massachusetts. A cluster of children that drank the water developed leukemia. Numerous epidemiological studies demonstrated increased rates of leukemia in persons exposed to TCE. The plaintiffs' attorney considered this to be conclusive evidence that the children's leukemia was caused by exposure to TCE. However, although TCE can cause leukemia, the problem with this conclusion is that it is not the only cause of leukemia. Benzene can cause leukemia. Children exposed to radiation can develop leukemia. Many times children develop leukemia for no known reason. Sometimes there is a cluster of children that develop leukemia for no known reason. Therefore, while epidemiological evidence demonstrates that a population of persons exposed to TCE will have an excessive number of cases of leukemia, the conclusion that any given individual's leukemia was caused by their TCE exposure is not necessarily true. While it may be possible to arrive at a reliable conclusion as to the cause of a disease where there are multiple factors that are capable of causing the disease, it requires a fair amount of work and expertise. A qualified expert must analyze a host of factors. These factors include the prevalence of the disease in persons with similar demographic characteristics but without exposure to the substance in question, history of exposure to other risk factors for the disease, and the relative risk of disease development due to the exposures. This analysis can be done, but it takes considerable skill. Interesting examples of this type of analysis can be found in the case studies in Part Four of this book.

Toxicogenomics and Causation

In toxic tort litigation, a person is often claiming to have developed cancer or some other serious disease due to having been exposed to a particular substance. Determining if the exposure to the substance was the cause of the disease is often a central focus of the litigation. New technical abilities to determine genetic sequences combined with traditional epidemiological methods offers the promise of improved tools to determine whether or not a person's disease was caused by or aggravated by exposure to a particular chemical or other substance. Toxicogenomics is the area of research that combines evaluation of gene expression and toxicology to investigate the interaction between genes and environmental stressor as it relates to disease causation.[1,2] As the field advances, toxicogenomics may play an increasing role in toxic tort litigation.

The core of toxicogenomics is the ability to examine the human genome. A genome is the full complement of genes from an organism determined at the time of conception by the combination of maternal and paternal DNA. The human genome consists of approximately 3 billion base pairs of deoxyribonucleic acid. There is an approximately 0.1 percent variability in the DNA sequences between individuals. The identification of the variability of gene expression between individuals after exposure to various toxins serves as the basis of toxicogenomics.[1]

One tool used in toxicogenomics is the use of microarrays to determine which genes are activated (expressed) after exposure to various chemicals.[3,4,5] In this technology, thousands of gene copies can be placed on small glass chips to see if, after a subject is exposed to a substance, the products of gene expression from any of the tested genes are made. Patterns of gene expression can be compiled and compared in order to identify possible toxins. Another toxicogenomic tool is the seeking of genetic abnormalities after toxin exposures as possible biomarkers demonstrating exposure to a specific toxin.[6] The third tool of toxicogenomics is the linkage of genetic information with epidemiological techniques in the field of molecular epidemiology to seek genetic classes of increased suspectablity.[7]

In toxic tort litigation, the plaintiff usually attempts to prove causation of a disease due to a toxin exposure while the defense counters by introducing evidence of alternative causes for the disease other than the alleged toxin exposure. The plaintiff must show both general and specific causation. General causation is a showing that exposure to the substance can cause the disease from which the plaintiff is suffering. After general causation has been proved, the plaintiff must prove specific causation by demonstrating that the particular exposure experienced by the plaintiff caused the plaintiff's disease. Currently the issue of general causation is elucidated by epidemiological studies showing elevated rates of disease in exposed versus non-exposed groups. Proof of specific causation is usually made through expert testimony concerning the exposure and the likelihood that that exposure caused the disease rather than some other exposure or circumstance.

Attempts to establish general causation may be made by introducing microarray findings that certain gene expression patterns demonstrate that exposure to a particular substance can cause a particular disease. The toxic tort litigator must remember that gene expression does not necessarily indicate that the expressed gene or genes causes a particular disease.[9] However, the combination of toxicogenomics with molecular epidemiology may advance scientific consensus concerning general disease causation.

The presence of biomarkers may be introduced in an attempt to prove specific causation. Again, the presence of a biomarkers alone without conventional methodologies used by qualified medical and exposure experts may not be sufficient to prove specific causation.[9,10]

Toxicogenomics may be used in an attempt to establish exposure to a particular substance. For example, DNA damage has been detected in benzene exposed workers. However, the findings of the DNA damage measures have not found widespread acceptance as biomarkers of exposure or effect with benzene mediated disease.[11]

A hereditary difference within a single gene which occurs in more than one percent of the population is referred to as genetic polymorphism. These genetic variations can lead to increased risks of disease in exposure groups. For example, approximately 50 percent of the Caucasian population has a gene deletion for the enzyme glutathione S-tranferase M1. This gene deletion causes an increased risk of lung cancer. [12] Toxicogenomics combined with molecular epidemiology studies may elucidate genetic types at increased risk of disease due to various substance exposures. The ability to indentify persons at increased risk of disease after substance exposures due to their genetic makeup has implication in litigation involving claims concerning fear of cancer, medical monitoring, and failure to warn.[13]

Toxicogenomics and the related discipline of molecular epidemiology hold great promise in identifying causes of disease in various exposure groups. These new tools may find increasing roles in toxic tort litigation. It is the responsibility of the toxic tort litigator to know when the right tool is being used for the right job.

1. Casarett & Doull's Toxicology: The Basic Science of Poisons. Seventh Edition. © 2008 by the McGraw-Hill Companies, Inc. ISBN 978-0-07-47051-3. Page 37.
2. Waters MD, Fostel JM: Toxicogenomics and systems toxicology: Aims and prospects. Nat Rev Genet 5:936-948, 2004.
3. Hamadeh HK. Et al. An overview of Toxicogenomics. Curr. Issues Mol. Biol. (2002) 4:45-56.
4. Weis BK. Et al. Personalized Exposure Assessment: Promising Approaches for Human Environmental Health Research. Environ Health Perspect. 2005 Jul;113(7):840-8.
5. Boverhof DR, Zacharewski TR. Toxicogenics in risk assessment: applications and needs. Toxicol Sci. 2006 Feb;89(2):352-60.
6. Vineis P, Perera F. Molecular epidemiology and biomarkers in etiologic cancer research: the new in light of the old. Cancer Epidemiol Biomarkers Prev. 2007 Oct;16(10):1954-65
7. Collings FB, Vaidya VS. Novel technologies for the discovery and quantification of biomarkers of toxicity. Toxicology. 2008 Mar 20;245(3):167-74.
8. Casarett & Doull's Toxicology: The Basic Science of Poisons. Seventh Edition. © 2008 by the McGraw-Hill Companies, Inc. ISBN 978-0-07-47051-3. Page 115.
9. Pierce JR, Sexton T. Toxicogenomics: towards the Future of Toxic Tort Causation. North Carolina Journal of Law & Technology. Volume5, Issue 1; Fall 2003.
10. Casarett & Doull's Toxicology: The Basic Science of Poisons. Seventh Edition. © 2008 by the McGraw-Hill Companies, Inc. ISBN 978-0-07-47051-3. Page 1177.

11. Casarett & Doull's Toxicology: The Basic Science of Poisons. Seventh Edition. © 2008 by the McGraw-Hill Companies, Inc. ISBN 978-0-07-47051-3. Page 1010.
12. Casarett & Doull's Toxicology: The Basic Science of Poisons. Seventh Edition. © 2008 by the McGraw-Hill Companies, Inc. ISBN 978-0-07-47051-3. Page 27.
13. Redick TP. Twenty-first Century Toxicogenomics Meets Twentieth Century Mass Tort Precedent: Is There a Duty to Warn of a Hypothetical Harm to an "Eggshell" Gene? Washburn Law Journal. Vol. 42. Jun 203. Pages 547-74.

CHAPTER FIVE

DAMAGES IN TOXIC TORT LITIGATION

*He who injured you was either stronger or weaker. If he was weaker, spare
him; if he was stronger, spare yourself.*

Seneca
De ira III

*Injuries should all be done together in order that men may taste their
bitterness but a short time and be but little disturbed. Benefits ought to be
conferred a little at a time, that their flavor may be tasted better.*

Machiavelli
The Prince VIII

Damages in toxic tort litigation usually fall into two general categories. These
categories are economic and non-economic damages.

Economic Damages

Economic damages compensate the plaintiff for any monetary losses he may have
suffered. Economic damages include compensation for out-of-pocket expenses like
medical expenses and lost wages. Economic damages also include property damage
like the rehabilitation or replacement of a home that is heavily contaminated with
a toxin. In certain cases, the economic damages are relatively easy to estimate. The
replacement costs of a heavily contaminated piece of property can be estimated by
looking at comparable real-estate sales in the area. Other economic damages are more
difficult to estimate. Loss of future wages may require the analysis of an economist.
The experienced attorney is very familiar with these matters.

A circumstance that commonly arises in toxic tort litigation is the presence of
persons that have been exposed to a toxic substance but are not currently ill. This

happens because many toxic substances do not cause manifestation of disease until many years after exposure. For example, a person exposed to asbestos usually does not develop lung cancer for decades after the exposure. Does this mean that the exposed person must wait twenty or thirty years until he develops lung cancer before he is able to file suit to collect damages? If this is so, then what about any lapse of the statute of limitations? Also, since asbestos is not the only cause of lung cancer, how is causation to be proved? This is difficult because other causes of lung cancer may be implicated, such as exposure to first or second-hand cigarette smoke. One answer to this question is to look for damages that may arise from toxin exposures other than those damages that are a consequence of present manifestation of disease. These damages include those that arise from the increased risk of disease due to the toxin exposure. Damages of this type present less of a causation problem since there should be strong support from the epidemiological literature to support the causal connection. For example, a man is exposed to a large quantity of inhaled asbestos due to the negligence of another person. He is not currently ill. The peer reviewed medical literature, backed by numerous epidemiological studies, strongly supports the assertion that the man is at increased risk of developing serious disease, including lung cancer, due to his exposure to asbestos. It may be difficult to establish a causal connection between his negligent exposure to asbestos and his subsequent development of lung cancer thirty years from now. However, it is clear that he has an increased risk of developing serious disease, including lung cancer, due to his asbestos exposure.

What are the damages that arise from an increased risk of disease? The first form of damages that arise from increased risk of disease is medical monitoring. The following is an example of medical monitoring:

A man is exposed to a toxic chemical that is known to cause an increased risk of serious disease. His exposure to the toxic chemical is in a sufficient amount and for a sufficient duration to cause him to have an increased risk of the development of serious disease. There is evidence that the man would benefit from improved survival if serious disease were detected early while effective treatment would still be possible. Medical monitoring is the course of periodic medical examinations and testing that are designed to detect his disease early while it is still treatable.

The expense of medical monitoring may be great given the high cost of medical diagnostic examinations and testing. Charges of $2,000 per year or more are often not unreasonable. A forty-year-old white man has a current expectation of additional years of life of 36.4 years *(Statistical Abstract of the United States. 119ᵗʰ Edition. 1999. U.S. Department of Commerce. Page 94)*. This amounts to lifetime medical monitoring expenses of $72,800 if the annual cost of medical monitoring is $2,000. Medical monitoring expenses can be considerable if there is a large class of plaintiffs, as may occur in a mass toxic tort case, or when there are children with long expectations of additional years of life.

Recovery of medical monitoring expenses as future consequential damages of increased risk of disease due to a toxin exposure have been considered and allowed in a number of jurisdictions throughout the United States. Medical monitoring expenses have been considered in Michigan in the case of *Meyerhoff v Turner Construction Co, 210 Mich. App. 491, 495, 534 N.W. 2d 204, 206 (1995)*. In Meyerhoff, the Court of Appeals ruled that *"medical monitoring expenses are a compensable form of damages where the proofs demonstrate that such surveillance to monitor the effect of exposure to toxic substances, such as asbestos, is reasonable and necessary."* The court then enumerated factors to be considered in determining whether they are reasonable and necessary. *Id.* These factors are: (1) the significance and extent of the exposure; (2) the toxicity of the substance; (3) the seriousness of the diseases for which the individuals are at risk; (4) the relative increase in the chance of onset of disease in those exposed; and (5) the value of early diagnosis. This is the same test for medical monitoring that was earlier applied in *Ayers v. Township of Jackson, 106 N.J. 557, 525 A. 2d 287 (1987)*. The Third Federal Circuit interpreted Pennsylvania law in *In re Paoli Railroad Yard PCB Litigation, 916 F. 2d 829 (1990)* as requiring plaintiffs seeking medical monitoring expenses to prove the following elements to a reasonable degree of medical certainty: (1) plaintiff was significantly exposed to a proven hazardous substance through the negligent actions of the defendant; (2) as a proximate result of exposure, plaintiff suffers an increased risk of contracting a serious latent disease; (3) that increased risk makes periodic diagnostic medical examinations reasonably necessary; (4) monitoring and testing procedures exist which make the early detection and treatment of the disease possible and beneficial. *(Gerald W. Boston and M. Stuart Madden. Law of Environmental and Toxic Torts: Cases, Materials and Problems. 1994 West Publishing Co. St. Paul, Minn. Page 186. Jean Macchiaroli Eggen. Toxic Torts in a Nutshell. 1995. West Publishing Co. St. Paul, Minn. pp. 213-22).*

It should be noted that on July 13, 2005, in *Gary and Kathy Henry, et al. v. The Dow Chemical Co., 473 Mich. 63*, the Michigan Supreme Court reversed its previous ruling in *Meyerhoff* and held that medical monitoring damages are not available in that State of Michigan.

While medical monitoring expenses compensate an individual for future costs involved in attempting to make an early diagnosis of serious disease arising from a toxin exposure, medical monitoring expenses do not cover the cost of treatment of disease once it has been diagnosed. This causes the serious dilemma of early knowledge of a serious disease, that could be cured if treated promptly, but for which there are no funds available from the tort-feasor for treatment.

An award of funds for treatment of all possible diseases that could arise from the toxin exposure would probably not be allowable since it is usually not certain that the exposed individual will develop any of the diseases known to arise from the toxin exposure. The solution is to award the cost of increased health insurance premiums due to the increased risk of disease arising from the toxin exposure. This is a new theory that is designed to cure the dilemma of diagnosis without treatment. *(Ernest P. Chiodo, Steve H. Huff, Donnelly W. Hadden. Increased Health, Lfe, and Disability Insurance Premium Costs: A New Class of Ecomonic Damages in Toxic Tort Cases in Michigan. 17 Mich Env L. J. No 3. pp 3-6).*

If medical monitoring expenses are allowable, as a consequence of the increased risk of disease arising from a toxin exposure, then compensation for increased health insurance premium costs should also be allowable as damages. Medical monitoring expenses are future damages arising from the increased risk of disease due to exposure. The increased risk is not a future event. It is a physical damage occurring at the cellular and sub-cellular level at the time of exposure. Medical monitoring expenses serve as only one possible form of future consequential damages arising from the central event of increased risk of disease. Increased insurance premiums are another form of future consequential damages arising from increased risk of disease with toxin exposure.

Under the common law in Michigan, any person who has been injured due to the acts or omissions of another is entitled to compensation in the form of monetary damages. The case of *Van Keulen & Winschester Lumber Co. v Manistee & NER Co, 222 Mich 682, 687, 193 NW 289, 290 (1923),* summarizes the common law of damages in Michigan:

> *The general rule of damages in an action of tort is that the wrong-doer is liable for all injuries resulting directly from the wrongful acts, whether they could or could not have been foreseen by him, provided the particular damages in respect to which he proceeds are the legal and natural consequences of the wrongful act imputed to the defendant, and are such as, according to common experience and the usual course of events, might reasonably have been anticipated. Remote, contingent, or speculative damages will not be considered in conformity to the general rule above laid down.*

This was also the holding in *Sutter v. Biggs*, 377 Mich 80, 86, 139 NW2d 684, 686 (1966).

Consequently, money damages to compensate a toxic exposure victim for any increase in insurance premiums due to increased risk of disease should be allowable in Michigan as long as they are not remote, contingent, or speculative.

Increased insurance premium costs, as a consequence of an increased risk of disease due to a toxin exposure, would in most circumstances fall into the category of future damages. The rule governing awards of future damages is set forth in *Brininstool v. Michigan United Ry Co., 157 Mich 172, 180, 121 NW 728, 731 (1909).*

> *It is the generally accepted rule that to entitle a plaintiff to recover damages presently for apprehended future consequences of an injury, there must be such a degree of probability of such consequences as to amount to reasonable certainty that they will result from the original injury.*

See also *Kellom v City of Ecorse, 329 Mich 303, 308, 45 NW2d 293, 295 (1951).*

A diligent search did not reveal any cases in Michigan concerning increased insurance premiums as future damages. However, case law from other jurisdictions show a trend toward allowing compensation for increased risk of future injury as long as it can be shown to a reasonable degree of certainty that the defendant's wrongdoing created the increased risk. See *Anderson v. Golden, 279 Ill. App. 3d 398, 664 N.E. 2d 1137 (1996); Petriello v. Kalman, 215 Conn. 377, 576 A. 2d 474 (1990); Davis v. Graviss, 672 S.W. 2d 928 (Ky. 1984); Feist v. Sears, Roebuck & Co., 267 Ore. 402, 517 P. 2d 675 (1973); Schwegel v. Goldberg, 209 Pa. Super. 280, 228 A. 2d 405 (1967).* These courts have found that the increased risk is itself a present injury which should be as compensable as any other present injury.

Therefore under Michigan law, a victim of a toxic substance exposure should recover as money damages, the amount of increased insurance premiums that are reasonably certain to occur due to his increased risk of disease due to the exposure. The increased insurance premiums are consequential future damages arising from the toxic substance exposure. Recovery of increased insurance costs is similar to recovery of medical monitoring expenses and arises from the same central event of increased risk of disease due to a toxic substance exposure.

Premiums for health, life, and disability insurance are based upon the risk of disease in certain population groups. For example, cigarette smokers have an increased risk of disease due to exposure to the toxins in cigarette smoke. Consequently, cigarette smokers are charged higher premiums for health, life, and disability insurance than are non-smokers. Although in the case of cigarette smoking, the increased risk of disease due to toxin exposure may arguably be self-inflicted; it is a clear illustration of increased insurance premiums charged due to increased risk of disease from a toxic substance exposure. Similarly, victims of toxic substance exposures may be entitled to money damages equal to the sum of the increased future premiums for health, life and disability insurance.

In order to recover increased health, life, and disability insurance premiums as consequential future damages arising from a toxic substance exposure, the plaintiffs must present expert medical testimony that they have suffered an increased risk of disease due to their toxin exposure. The plaintiffs must then present testimony from an insurance expert that their increased risk of disease due to a toxin exposure is reasonably certain to result in increased insurance premiums. The insurance expert must also testify to the amount of the increased insurance premium so that the amount of future damages may be quantified. The amount of damages would be the expected years of life remaining for the exposed individual times the differential insurance premiums for the individual with and without the history of the toxic exposure. There is no need to reduce the amount to present value if there is competent expert testimony presented that the rates of interest on investments and the rates of inflation for health, life, and disability insurance premiums are likely to remain approximately equal.

The fact that an individual is not currently covered by health, life, or disability insurance should not preclude him from obtaining increased insurance premiums as future damages. The analogy here to medical monitoring expenses is clear. An individual need not show that he is engaged in a medical monitoring program in order to obtain medical monitoring costs as future damages. Similarly, a toxic exposure victim with current insurance coverage need not show that his insurance premiums have been increased due to the exposure. The fact that his insurance premiums have not increased may merely be a manifestation of his insurance carrier having not yet learned of the exposure or having not yet appreciated the increased risk of disease due to the exposure. All that is required is that expert testimony be presented stating that it is reasonably certain that his insurance premiums will increase due to his toxin exposure.

Whenever a new theory is proposed, consideration must be made as to why the theory did not arise before. In the case of future damages for increased insurance premiums due to a toxic substance exposure, there are two factors that may explain why this theory did not arise previously. The first factor is that this new theory is a derivative of increased risk of disease due to exposure. The birth of this theory, like its sister theory of medical monitoring expenses, had to await the development of scientific knowledge of increased risk of disease arising from cellular and sub-cellular damage due to toxic substance exposures. The second factor may be reluctance on the part of many attorneys to refer to insurance during the course of litigation. This may have arisen from the prohibition against the admission of evidence of liability insurance for the purpose of showing that another party acted negligently. MRE 411 states the following:

> *Evidence that a person was or was not insured against liability is not admissible upon the issue whether the person acted negligently or otherwise wrongfully. This rule does not require the exclusion of evidence of insurance against liability when offered for another purpose, such as proof of agency, ownership, or control, if controverted, or bias or prejudice of a witness.*

While evidence of increased premiums for health, life, and disability insurance is not prohibited by MRE 411, the involvement of insurance may have paralyzed other proponents of medical monitoring expenses from recognizing this new theory. Increased insurance premiums are at their core only another future consequential damage arising from increased risk of disease due to a toxin exposure.

It should be emphasized that it is not proposed that the tort-feasor bear the total cost of health, life, and disability insurance. What is proposed is that the tort-feasor pays only the increased premium costs resulting from the increased risk of disease due to the toxin exposure. However, it is conceivable that in some circumstances an argument may be made that the tort-feasor bear the entire cost of insurance if the insurance would not have been necessary without the occurrence of the toxic substance exposure.

Defendants in a toxic tort action may raise the availability of insurance through health maintenance organizations. It may be argued that health maintenance organizations licensed in the State of Michigan must charge the same premiums for individuals without regard to their risk of disease. Therefore, a victim of a toxic substance exposure would not experience an increase in the premiums for health coverage through a health maintenance organization. The defendant will then argue that even if the victim of a toxic substance exposure can show that he would experience an increase in the premiums of conventional health insurance, he does not have a valid claim since he may purchase a health maintenance organization policy at no increased cost. This final argument is incorrect. Concerns about limited access to necessary care with health maintenance organizations have reached the level of common knowledge. There is a perception that coverage by a health maintenance organization provides second-class health care. While this perception may be false in many cases, there is no reason to require a person to limit his choice of health coverage to an HMO merely because he has been the victim of a toxin exposure.

It is clear that the expenses for medical monitoring and increased insurance premiums are future damages that are both derived from the increased risk of disease due to a toxic substance exposure. However, it is reasonable to ask whether a toxic substance exposure victim may recover both medical monitoring expenses and increased insurance premium costs. Should this be barred as a double recovery?

In the case of increased life and disability insurance premiums, there is clearly no double recovery since these insurance products do not involve coverage for health care services. In the case of health care insurance, there may at first glance be a risk of double recovery since health care insurance and medical monitoring expenses involve recovery for health care services. However, these concerns are relieved with a deeper analysis. Medical monitoring expenses only cover screening for the early detection of serious disease, the prompt treatment of which would improve the chances of survival. However, medical monitoring expenses do not cover treatment of disease. An award of medical monitoring expenses leaves the victim of a toxic substance exposure with a terrible dilemma. He is provided funds for the early detection of disease so that he may benefit from increased survival through the prompt treatment of disease. However, he is not provided with resources for the treatment necessary to improve his survival. The victim of a toxic substance exposure is provided no net benefit from medical monitoring since without treatment he has no increased survival due to the early detection of disease. The solution of this dilemma can not be the provision of funds for treatment since it is not certain that disease will occur. Rather, the solution is to provide funds to cover any increase in health insurance premiums resulting from the increased risk of disease due to a toxin exposure. With this relief, health insurance will be available to provide treatment of any disease that the medical monitoring is designed to detect. Therefore, it is obvious that payment of both medical monitoring expenses and increased health insurance premiums is not a double recovery. They are each separate, but necessary, components of a plan geared to improve survival of persons with a toxic substance exposure.

The above discussion about the dual need for medical monitoring for early detection of curable toxin caused disease, and the availability of treatment to cure the disease, brings focus upon another argument for allowance of increased health insurance premiums as future consequential damages. This argument centers upon the remedies provided to individuals in Michigan suffering a toxic substance exposure in the workplace. Under section 315(1) of the Worker's Disability Compensation Act of 1969, an employer shall furnish reasonable medical treatment to an injured worker including *"medical, surgical, and hospital services and medicines, or other attendance or treatment recognized by the laws of this state as legal, when they are needed."* Worker's compensation provides a worker suffering increased risk of disease due to a toxic substance exposure access to both medical monitoring and treatment. Victims of toxic substance exposures outside of the workplace only have access to medical monitoring but not treatment without allowance for recovery of increased premium costs for health insurance. There is no apparent reason why a worker suffering a toxin exposure should have better access to resources leading to improved survival than does an individual suffering an exposure outside of the work place.

In conclusion, increased insurance premiums should be allowable future consequential damages in the State of Michigan in cases of toxic substance exposures. These future consequential damages arise from the increased risk of disease due to a toxic substance exposure. The increased risk of disease with a toxic substance exposure is the common origin of the separate future damages of medical monitoring expenses and increased insurance premium costs. Allowance of increased insurance premiums, as future damages, is necessary to achieve the medical monitoring goal of improved survival for toxic substance exposure victims. In addition to attempting to make toxic substance exposure victims whole, increased insurance premium costs combine with medical monitoring expenses to serve the important public policy goal of deterring potential tort-feasors in toxic tort actions by making them bear the full cost of the damages arising from their activities.

Non-Economic Damages

The litigator must be aware of a special class of economic damages that arise in toxic tort cases. These damages are in compensation for the fear of cancer or other serious diseases that may arise from a toxic substance exposure. In Michigan, the lead case allowing recovery for fear of cancer or serious disease is *Stites v. Sunderstrand Heat Transfer, Inc., 660 F. Supp. 1516, 1527 (W.D. Mich. 1987), 2 Toxics L Rep (BNA) 681 (1987)*. In order to recover, the plaintiff must demonstrate some present manifestation of disease attributable to their exposure, or to the anxiety arising from their exposure. This is consistent with section 436A of the Restatement 2nd of Torts which proposes the following general rule: *"If the actor's conduct is negligent as creating an unreasonable risk of causing either bodily harm or emotional disturbance to another, and it results in such emotional disturbance alone, without bodily harm or other compensable damage, the actor is not liable for such emotional disturbance."* However, in *Potter v. Firestone Tire and Rubber Co., 25 Cal. Rptr. 2d 550, 863 P. 2d 795 (1993)*, the California Supreme Court allowed a claim for negligent infliction of emotional distress in the absence of physical injury and stated the following:

> *The physical injury requirement is a hopelessly imprecise screening device—it would allow recovery for fear of cancer whenever such distress accompanies or results in any physical injury, no matter how trivial, yet would disallow recovery*

in all cases where the fear is both serious and genuine but no physical injury has yet manifested itself.

(Jean Macchiaroli Eggen. Toxic Torts in a Nutshell. 1995. West Publishing Co. St. Paul, Minn. Page 235)

If the conduct that resulted in the toxin exposure was outrageous, the plaintiff may bring an action to recover damages for emotion distress. The Restatement 2nd of Torts, § 46 (1965) recognizes a tort of outrageous conduct causing severe emotional distress. In *Capital Holding Corp. v. Bailey, 873 S.W. 2d 187 (Ky. 1994)*, the court allowed an outrageous conduct claim to stand due to the defendant knowingly and recklessly exposing the plaintiff to asbestos.

Of course, the reader is reminded to review the case law listed above with particular attention to any changes that may have occurred.

MEDICAL MONITORING DAMAGES

By

Dan Breen

You can never plan the future by the past.

Edmund Burke

Generally

M edical monitoring is periodic testing and/or examination to facilitate the diagnosis and treatment of a latent disease by early detection. Medical monitoring damages are necessary in cases when, in the absence of physical injury, the plaintiff should be able to recover the cost for various diagnostic examinations proximately caused by the defendant's negligent conduct.[1]

As discussed in *Friends for All Children, Inc. v. Lockheed Aircraft Corp.*, medical monitoring damages are driven by two basic ideals of tort law because "allowing recovery for the expense of diagnostic examinations recommended by competent physicians will, in theory, deter misconduct." (in toxic tort cases, this compels parties to minimize the risks and costs of exposure). The idea of medical monitoring claims accord "with commonly shared intuitions of normative justice which underlie the common law of tort. [A defendant], through his own negligence, caused the plaintiff, in the opinion of medical experts, to need specific medical services—a cost that is neither inconsequential nor of the kind the community generally accepts as part of the wear and tear of daily life."[2] Accordingly, the defendant can only make the plaintiff whole by paying for the necessary medical services. 746 F. 2d 816 (D.C. Cir. 1984).

"A claim for a medical monitoring fund is significantly different from a claim for a lump-sum award of damages. A trust fund compensates a plaintiff for only the monitoring costs actually incurred. In contrast, a lump-sum award of damages is a monetary award that the plaintiff can spend as he or she sees fit. Because the plaintiffs in this case are seeking the establishment of a judicially supervised fund to administer their medical surveillance payments, we offer no opinion concerning whether lump-sum damages are recoverable under Louisiana law."[3]

Other policy considerations include the fact that medical monitoring promotes early diagnosis and treatment of disease resulting from a tortfeasor's negligence.

Second, allowing recovery for such expenses avoids the potential injustice of forcing an economically disadvantaged person to pay for expensive diagnostic examinations and affords victims, for whom other sorts of recovery may prove difficult, immediate compensation for medical monitoring needed as a result of exposure. Third, such recovery is in harmony with the important public health interest in fostering access to medical testing for individuals whose injuries/exposure creates an inherent risk of disease and/or future manifestation of an injury.[4]

While the law of medical monitoring is evolving, and there are slight variations in the way different jurisdictions set forth the elements of a medical monitoring claim, the most common elements of a medical monitoring claim are:

1. The plaintiff was significantly exposed to a proven hazardous substance through the negligent actions of the defendant.
2. As a proximate result of exposure, the plaintiff suffers a significantly increased risk of contracting a serious latent disease.
3. That increased risk makes periodic diagnostic medical examinations reasonably necessary.
4. Monitoring and testing procedures exist which make the early detection and treatment of the disease possible and beneficial.
5. A reasonable physician would prescribe for the plaintiff a monitoring regime different than the one that would have been prescribed in the absence of that particular exposure.[5]

Illinois' Position

Inasmuch as Illinois' Supreme Court has not ruled specifically on medical monitoring, this area of law remains in development. That being said, appellate courts and federal courts interpreting Illinois law support recovery for medical monitoring, most notably in the absence of present physical injury, but *Jensen v. Bayer AG* 371 Ill. App. 3d 682 (1 Dist. 2007) and *Lewis v. Lead Indus. Ass'n*, 342 Ill. App. 3d 95 (1 Dist. 2003), are permissive of medical monitoring under the following rationale:

> There is a fundamental difference between a claim seeking damages for an increased risk of future harm and one which seeks compensation for the cost of medical examinations. The injury which is alleged, and for which compensation is sought, in a claim seeking damages for an increased risk of harm is the anticipated harm itself. The injury which is alleged, and for which compensation is sought, in a claim seeking damages for a medical

examination to detect a possible physical injury is the cost of the examination. Unlike a claim seeking damages for an increased risk of future harm, a claim seeking damages for the cost of a medical examination is not speculative and the necessity for such an examination is capable of proof within a "reasonable degree of medical certainty." If a defendant's breach of duty makes it necessary for a plaintiff to incur expenses to determine if he or she has been physically injured, we find no reason why the expense of such an examination is any less a present injury compensable in a tort action than the medical expenses that might be incurred to treat an actual physical injury caused by such a breach of duty.

The court in Courts in *Carey v. Kerr-McGee Chemical Corp*[6] determined that a claim for medical monitoring to detect the onset of physical harm in the absence of any showing of present physical harm would not conflict with Illinois law, if the Illinois Supreme Court were to hear the issue. Carey further stated that the appropriate inquiry for such a claim would be whether "medical monitoring is, to a reasonable degree of medical certainty, necessary in order to diagnose properly the warning signs of disease."

As such, medical monitoring damages are permitted in Illinois without a present physical injury. Carey stands for the proposition that if faced with the precise issue before that court, the Illinois Supreme Court would uphold a claim for medical monitoring without requiring plaintiffs to plead and prove either a present physical injury of a reasonable certainty of contracting a disease in the future.[7]

The Future of Medical Monitoring Damages in Illinois

The to uphold an award of medical monitoring damages was *Friends for All Children, Inc. v. Lockheed Aircraft Corp.* Because any recognition of a cause of action for medical monitoring began under years prior to this writing, legal analysis of situations that necessitate medical monitoring damages remains in the early stages. This is true in Illinois and across the country.

As mentioned above, the justifications and policy that underscore the growing need for widespread recognition of medical monitoring damages are apparent. The challenges are how to implement and administer an advanced and different form of damages than traditional tort law has handled. Keep in mind that a core ideal of our current paradigm is the 200 year old tort principle that did not allow a plaintiff to recover without proof of a physical injury.[8] In a case before the Supreme Court requesting medical monitoring in an asbestos case, Justice Breyer noted the "potential systemic effects of creating a new, full-blown tort law cause of action—for example, the effects upon the interests of other potential plaintiffs who are not before the court and who depend on a tort system that can distinguish between reliable and serious claims on the one hand, and unreliable and relatively trivial claims on the other hand."[9]

Another concern includes limiting medical monitoring damages to cases where injury is not speculative and opponents would justifiably like to ensure that recovery is prohibited in cases of incurable disease.[10] Further concerns are laid out as follows:

> Implementation and administration of a sound plan would require, at a minimum, specifying the nature and amount of benefits available, the source of funding and funding allotments, the procedures for determining eligibility for monitoring, when eligible parties may join the program, how long the program should last, and how long it should be implemented. *See* Jesse R. Lee, *Medical Monitoring Damages: Issues Concerning the Administrations of Medical Monitoring Programs*, 20 Am. J.L. & Med. 251, 267-72 (1994). Moreover, as the program matures, its scope and administrative operation inevitably will require adjustments, especially if the program's designers erroneously estimate funding needs or the number of eligible participants. For example, a court-guided trust set up to administer asbestos claims against the Johns-Manville Company "settled 25,000 our of more than 140,000 claims [before] deplet[ing] its funds.[11]

Some authorities have noted that the legislatures assistance is vital in crafting a sound medical monitoring policy. Legislature are well equipped to reach fully informed decisions about the need for widespread changes in the law because "An appropriate cost-benefit analysis in the context of medical monitoring requires the decision maker to consider a host of detailed and intricately intertwined factors that courts may not have the resources to formulate or weigh."[12] Further, "Prospective legislative consideration of medical monitoring would give the public advance notice of significant changes affecting the rights and duties, and the time to comport behavior accordingly."[13] "Legislatures . . . not only have the requisite authority to confront and resolve the broad public policy issues raised by medical monitoring, but they also have the tools necessary to do so in a sound manner—access to nearly limitless sources of information and the ability to initiate legislation prospectively. In short, tackling the challenges inherent in allowing awards for medical monitoring ought to be left to legislatures rather than decided by courts."[14]

Medical monitoring damages will pave their way forward and evolve into complex disputes for the next generation of litigation. While the courts have acted where their action has been necessitated thus far, it remains to be seen whether this unique remedy will continue to be crafted by the courts or of the legislature will devise a regimented distribution scheme.

Endnotes

1. Herbert L. Zarov, Sheila Finnegan, Craig A. Woods, and Stephen J. Kane, *A Medical Monitoring Claim For Asymptomatic Plaintiffs: Should Illinois Take the Plunge?*, 12 DePaul J. Health Care L. 1, 4 (2009).
2. 746 F. 2d 816 (D.C. Cir. 1984).
3. *Bourgeois v. AP Green industries, Inc.*, 716 So. 2d 355 at 357 n. 3.
4. Turner W. Branch and Margaret Moses Branch, *Environmental Tort Litigation*, 6 Litigating Tort Cases §67:24 Medical Monitoring (2009).
5. *Id.*
6. 999 F. Supp. 1109, 1119-20 (N.D. Ill. 1998).
7. *Id.*
8. Victor E. Schwartz, Mark A. Behrens, Emma K. Burton and Jennifer L Groninger, *Medical Monitoring—Should Tort Law Say Yes?*, 34 Wake Forest L. Rev. 1057 (1999).
9. *Metro—North CommuterR.R. Co. v. Buckley*, 521 U.S. 424 (1997).
10. 34 Wake Forest L. Rev. 1057.
11. Judicial Conference Ad Hoc Committee on Asbestos Litigation, Report of the Ad Hoc Committee 25 (1991).
12. 34 Wake Forest L. Rev. 1057.
13. *Id.*
14. *Id.*

CHAPTER SEVEN

EXPERT WINTESSES

More is experienced in one day in the life of a learned man than in the
whole lifetime of an ignorant man.

Seneca

Epistolae LXXVIII

The difference between winning and losing toxic tort cases focuses largely upon arranging for qualified expert testimony. There are many types of experts that come to play a role in toxic tort litigation. There are physicians with various areas of specialization. There are industrial hygienists. There are epidemiologists. There are toxicologists. There are statisticians. There are environmental engineers. The list goes on and on. This book can not discuss all the various types of experts that may be called upon to testify in a toxic tort action. However, the strengths and weaknesses of the most frequently utilized experts will be considered.

In general, it is best to use the smallest possible number of expert witnesses necessary to make or defend your case. The more experts you have, the more expense that you will incur for yourself and your client. You will also run the risk of multiple experts contradicting each other in subtle but important ways.

Physicians

There are over 800,000 physicians in the United States. Many of these physicians are board certified in some specialty; however, what does it mean to be board certified? When the term "board certified" is used in reference to a physician, it is usually meant that the physician is certified by one of the American Board of Medical Specialties (ABMS) boards. These are the boards that hospitals consider when determining whether a physician has proper credentials to serve on staff. The ABMS boards consist of twenty-three specialty boards including: the American Board of Internal Medicine; the American Board of Surgery; the American Board of Pediatrics; and the American

Board of Preventive Medicine. The American Board of Preventive Medicine grants board certification in three areas of specialization. These are (1) aerospace medicine; (2) public health and general preventive medicine; and (3) occupational medicine. Specialists in aerospace medicine are the types of physicians that serve on the staff of NASA. Specialist in public health and general preventive medicine are the types of physicians that serve as medical directors of state and local health departments or work for the Centers for Disease Control (CDC). Specialists in occupational medicine (occupational and environmental medicine) are the physicians that specialize in the diagnosis, treatment, and prevention of diseases caused by work place and environmental exposures. This includes exposure to toxic substances at work or in the environment. Board certified occupational and environmental medicine physicians are usually the appropriate physician expert witnesses in toxic tort cases. It is possible for a physician to gain expertise concerning exposure, causation, and risk of disease due to a toxin exposure and not be board certified in occupational and environmental medicine; however, it is rare. In addition to going to medical school, the board certified occupational and environmental medicine physician has usually attended public health school. In public health school, the board certified occupational and environmental medicine physician has usually received formal training in biostatistics, epidemiology, and toxicology. Knowledge of these disciplines is essential for the formation of expert testimony in toxic tort cases. This knowledge is not emphasized during the training of most physicians. As a result, it is dangerous for either the plaintiff or defense to develop their case without the consultation and availability for testimony of an expert physician, board certified in occupational and environmental medicine.

The occupational and environmental medicine expert should assist the attorney in determining the necessity of other experts and the need for environmental testing. Preconceived notions on the part of the attorney about the need for testing, without the advice of an occupational and environmental medicine physician, can be an expensive mistake.

Since a well-qualified occupational and environmental medicine physician will have formal training and academic course work in toxicology, in addition to credentials in clinical medicine, it is often unnecessary to use a non-physician toxicologist as an expert. In addition to incurring unnecessary expense, and the risk of two of the attorney's own experts providing contradictory testimony, the danger of using a non-physician toxicologist is demonstrated by the following line of cross examination questioning:

Q: Sir, am I correct that your name is Dr. X? (Addressed to a non—physician toxicologist).

A: Yes, that is my name.

Q: What type of doctor are you?

A: I am a doctor of toxicology.

Q: Doctor, you gave an opinion that the chemical my client was exposed to could not have caused his disease, isn't that so?

A: Yes.

Q: Now doctor, you are not a medical doctor, are you?

A: Yes.

Q: You are a Ph.D. doctor?

A: Yes.

Q: Doctor, are you licensed to practice medicine in this state?

A: No.

Q: Are you licensed to practice medicine anywhere in the United States?

A: No.

Q: So, if I came to see you with a sore throat, you would not be licensed
To treat me?

A: Yes.

Q: Nor would you be licensed to treat me if I had any other medical or surgical disease.

A: Yes.

While the above line of questioning may not completely discredit the expert in the eyes of the jury, it does show the danger of using a non-physician expert toxicologist. While non-physician experts in engineering or industrial hygiene may be suitable, toxicology is too close to medicine. A jury is likely to expect that an expert in toxicology be a "real" doctor qualified to treat patients.

The same concerns apply to a lesser extent to non-physician experts in epidemiology and biostatistics. These are disciplines that are close enough to medicine that a jury may expect the expert to be a qualified physician. However, the mathematical character of these disciplines may make testimony by a non-physician expert more acceptable to a jury than in the case of toxicology. Again, it should be remembered that these are disciplines that are included in the training and expertise of a well-qualified occupational and environmental medicine physician. Consequently, the use of multiple experts, in addition to the occupational and environmental medicine physician, in matters concerning epidemiology or bio-statistics may be an expensive mistake.

Industrial Hygienists

Industrial hygienists are the professionals that conduct sampling and monitoring of toxic substances in the workplace and the environment. The American Board of Industrial Hygiene grants certification to industrial hygienists with the designation of C.I.H. (Certified Industrial Hygienist). Most industrial hygienists came into the field with a background in an engineering or chemical discipline. It is frequently helpful to have an industrial hygienist involved as an expert in a toxic substance case. The role of the industrial hygienist is to obtain samples in order to quantify the amount of exposure to the toxic substance. This then helps build the foundation of the testimony of the occupational and environmental medicine physician whom then testifies as to the effects on human health of the exposure. This provides a seamless line of testimony with a solid foundation for the amount of toxin exposure and its consequences. This is the good one-two punch that the plaintiff or defense attorney needs in many toxic tort cases.

Other Experts

Experts in other disciplines are commonly needed in toxic substances litigation. A hydrologist is frequently needed in order to describe and quantify the extent of ground water contamination. A civil and environmental engineer may be required to testify about the cause of sewer intrusions. A building inspector may be required to examine a home for construction defects in circumstances of mold contamination. A realtor may be needed to document decreased real-estate values due to environmental contamination. The need for these experts is dependent upon the circumstances occurring in each case. It is obviously important when using experts to obtain those with the best available professional education and experience. Accreditation with a recognized professional organization is important. It is often helpful to gain advice as to the necessity of other experts from your occupational and environmental medicine and industrial hygiene experts. These professionals can be very helpful in helping the attorney determine what types of experts are needed in the case.

One final word of warning is in order concerning expert witnesses in the age of Daubert. Judges, in their role as gatekeepers, are charged with preventing junk science from reaching juries. It is important to select experts that are capable of surviving a Daubert challenge. Daubert has necessitated plaintiffs and defendants to obtain better-qualified and more careful experts that may have been required in the past.

CHAPTER EIGHT

DAUBERT RULES LIMITING EXPERT WITNESS TESTIMONY

We also are compassed about with so great a cloud of witnesses.

Hebrews 12:1

Prior to the Daubert line of cases, the evidentiary rule that applied in federal courts concerning admissibility of expert testimony was the Frye Doctrine. The holding in Frye was that *"While courts will go a long way in admitting expert testimony deduced from a well-recognized scientific principle or discovery, the thing from which the deduction is made must be sufficiently established to have gained general acceptance in the particular field in which it belongs."*

After the adoption of the Federal Rules of Evidence in 1975, the courts began to stray from the Frye "general acceptance" rule. This was caused in part by Rule 402 of the Federal Rules, which made all relevant evidence admissible with the limitation of Rule 403; that excludes evidence in which the probative value is substantially out-weighed by its prejudicial effect. In 1993, the United States Supreme Court decided in Daubert v. Merrell Dow Pharmaceuticals, Inc. that under the Federal Rules of Evidence, the trial judge must ensure that any scientific testimony or evidence admitted is not only relevant but reliable. The Supreme Court established factors that the trial court must consider in making its determination that the expert testimony is reliable. First, the trial court must consider whether or not the scientific technique or theory has been tested. Second, the trial court must determine whether or not a study has been published or has undergone some other form of peer review. Thirdly, the court must determine whether or not there is an error rate associated with the scientific technique used. Finally, the court must determine whether the theory offered is generally accepted in the relevant scientific community. *(Jean Macchiaroli Eggen. Toxic Torts in a Nutshell. 1995. West Publishing Co. St. Paul, Minn. pp 213-22)*

The Daubert factors require that experts carefully formulate and prepare their opinions. Gone are the days of expert testimony being admitted solely because the proponent possesses a curriculum vitae with impressive credentials. It is important that an expert be able to support the essential points of his opinion with the peer reviewed scientific literature. In addition, the expert should cite the relevant peer reviewed literature articles in his report. This protects the admissibility of his opinion as an expert as well as demonstrates the strength of his opinion.

The essence of Daubert has been statutorily adopted in the State of Michigan. M.C.L.A. 600. 2955 reads as follows:

1. *In an action for the death of a person or for injury to a person or property, a scientific opinion rendered by an otherwise qualified expert is not admissible unless the court determines that the opinion is reliable and will assist the trier of fact. In making that determination, the court shall examine the opinion and the basis for the opinion, which basis includes the facts, technique, methodology, and reasoning relied on by the expert, and shall consider all of the following factors:*

    a. *Whether the opinion and its basis have been subjected to scientific testing and replication.*

    b. *Whether the opinion and its basis have been subjected to peer review publication.*

    c. *The existence and maintenance of generally accepted standards governing the application and interpretation of a methodology or technique and whether the opinion and its basis are consistent with those standards.*

    d. *The known or potential error rate of the opinion and its basis.*

    e. *The degree to which the opinion and its basis are generally accepted within the relevant expert community. As used in this subdivision, "relevant expert community" means individuals who are knowledgeable in the field of study and are gainfully employed applying that knowledge on the free market.*

    f. *Whether the basis for the opinion is reliable and whether experts in that field would rely on the same basis to reach the type of opinion being proffered.*

    g. *Whether the opinion or methodology is relied upon by experts outside of the context of litigation.*

2. *A novel methodology or form of scientific evidence may be admitted into evidence only if its proponent establishes that it has achieved general scientific acceptance among impartial and disinterested experts in the field.*

3. *In an action alleging medical malpractice, the provisions of this section are in addition to, and do not otherwise affect, the criteria for expert testimony provided in section 2165.*

However, the toxic tort attorney should research the existence of Daubert type evidence rules in state actions that he is engaged in or is considering.

It is often prudent to have an affidavit from your expert witness on hand to counter any stated or federal Daubert challenges. The following is an example of an affidavit from an occupational and environmental medicine physician. The provisions of M.C.L.A. 600. 2955 are incorporated into the affidavit.

AFFIDAVIT OF XXXXXX M.D., M.P.H

STATE OF MICHIGAN   )
)   SS
COUNTY OF WAYNE   )

XXXXXX M.D., M.P.H., being duly sworn states as follows:

1. *That I am a physician licensed to practice medicine in the State of Michigan.*
2. *The American Board of Preventive Medicine certifies me in the specialty of occupational medicine.*
3. *That I am qualified to render opinions concerning the existence and cause of disease in persons exposed to unhealthy conditions in the workplace and the environment.*
4. *That I examined John and Mary Doe in my clinical office on February 1, 2002.*
5. *That my curriculum vitae is attached to this affidavit.*
6. *That I believe that my opinion is reliable and would assist a trier of fact.*
7. *That my expert opinion in this matter is grounded upon recognized scientific knowledge that has been subjected to scientific testing and replication.*
8. *That my expert opinion and its basis are consistent with the peer-reviewed scientific literature, and if called upon I would be able to provide cites from the peer-reviewed scientific literature that corroborate my opinion.*
9. *That generally accepted standards exist and are maintained within the occupational medicine expert community concerning the application and interpretation of methodologies and techniques used in occupational medicine practice and my opinion is consistent with those standards.*
10. *That I am able to provide a known or potential error rate of my opinion and its basis.*
11. *That I believe that my opinion would be generally accepted within the community of occupational medicine physicians who are knowledgeable in the field of study and are gainfully employed in applying that knowledge on the free market.*
12. *That the basis of my opinion in this matter is reliable and experts in occupational medicine would rely upon the same basis to reach the type of opinion being proffered.*
13. *That my opinion and methodology is consistent with the type of opinion and methodology relied upon by experts outside of the confines of litigation.*

14. *That I believe that my opinion is not novel and would be generally accepted among impartial and disinterested experts in the field of occupational medicine.*
15. *That in my opinion John and Mary Doe have suffered respiratory symptoms due to their exposure to asbestos.*
16. *That in my opinion John and Mary Doe are at increased risk of suffering serious disease including mesothelioma, lung cancer, asbestosis, and renal cancer due to their exposure to asbestos.*
17. *That in my opinion John and Mary Doe will benefit from periodic medical monitoring for early detection of disease arising from their asbestos exposure.*
18. *Attached is a copy of my report dated February 15, 2002. In that report I provide my opinion and the basis of my opinion. I also provide cites from the peer reviewed medical and scientific literature that corroborates my opinion. Copies of the cited articles are attached to my report.*

Further, deponent sayeth not.

XXXXXXX, M.D., M.P.H.

Subscribed and sworn to before me this 1st day of March 2002.

When one thinks of toxic substances litigation, one usually thinks of toxic tort litigation. However, it is important not to forget that much of worker's compensation litigation involves workers claiming to have suffered illness due to exposure to toxic substances at work. It is rare for worker's compensation attorneys to raise a Daubert challenge to the admissibility of the opponent's expert. However, a Daubert style admissibility challenge may be effective in destroying the credibility of the opponent's non-conforming expert even if the worker's compensation magistrate allows admission of the testimony. Of course, in order for this approach to have a significant impact, the testimony of the challenging attorney's expert must be in compliance with Daubert. This is particularly effective in states, like Michigan, that have statutorily enacted Daubert type admissibility rules for expert testimony.

CHAPTER NINE

SOPHISTICATED USER DOCTRINE

In much wisdom is much grief: and he that increaseth
knowledge increaseth sorrow.

Ecclesiastes 1:18

The toxic tort attorney must be aware of the sophisticated user doctrine as it is applied in the State of Michigan. The sophisticated user doctrine usually arises in a situation where a worker is injured by a hazardous substance supplied by a third party to his employer. The employee's exclusive remedy against his employer is worker's compensation unless the employee can show that the employer intended to injure him (See Chapter Seven "Worker's Compensation as Exclusive Remedy"). Consequently, the worker frequently considers filing a third party toxic tort action against the manufacturer and the supplier of the hazardous product under a failure to warn theory. A toxic tort action against the manufacturer or the supplier may be barred by the sophisticated user doctrine.

In *Antcliff v State Employees Credit Union, 414 Mich. 624, 627; 327 N.W. 2d 814, 815 (1982)*, the Michigan Supreme Court considered the claim of the plaintiff against the manufacturer of a powered scaffold that unexpectedly gave way while he was standing on it. The Court examined the relationship between the manufacturer, architect, contractor, and credit union before it recognized what is now known as the "sophisticated user" doctrine. The facts in the case showed that the manufacturer of the powered scaffold only sold the product to professional riggers. In *Antcliff* at 640, the Court stated the following:

> *"There are countless skilled operations such as the rigging of scaffolding, which involve otherwise non-dangerous products in potentially dangerous situations. A manufacturer of such a product should be able to presume mastery of the basic operation. The more so when, as here, the manufacturer affirmatively and successfully limits the market of its product to professionals. In such a case, the*

manufacturer should not be burdened with the often difficult task of providing instructions on how to properly perform the basic operation."

In *Antcliff* at 630, the Court also held that *"a manufacturer's liability to a purchaser or a user of its product should be assessed with reference to whether its conduct, including the dissemination of information about the product, was reasonable under the circumstances."*

The Michigan Court of Appeals held in *Aetna Casualty & Surety Co v. Ralph Wilson Plastics Co., 202 Mich. App. 540, 546; 509 NW2d 520, 524 (1993)*, that *"commercial enterprises that use materials in bulk must be regarded as sophisticated users, as a matter of law."*

However, providers of materials in bulk to employers may lose their sophisticated user defense if they become engaged in practices that create a duty, including the duty to warn, to workers.

The toxic tort attorney should research the application of sophisticated user doctrine in their jurisdiction.

CHAPTER TEN

WORKER'S COMPENSATION AS EXCLUSIVE REMEDY

In order that people may be happy in their work, these three things are needed: They must be fit for it: They must not do too much of it: And they must have a sense of success in it.

John Ruskin
Pre-Raphaelitism

The workplace is frequently the scene of a toxin exposure. The Michigan Worker's Disability Compensation Act of 1969 provides injured workers with a system of benefits in a no-fault scheme. The primary purpose of the worker's compensation act is to provide benefits to workers that have suffered work related injuries through a system that places the burden of payments on employers. The system provides compensation regardless of fault to employees that have suffered injury arising out of their employment. *Eversman v. Concrete Cutting & Breaking, 463 Mich. 86, 92; 614 N.W. 2d 862, 864 (2000).*

Worker's compensation is usually the exclusive remedy. M.C.L.A. 418. 131(1) reads as follows:

The right to the recovery of benefits as provided in this act shall be the employee's exclusive remedy against the employer for a personal injury or occupational disease. The only exception to this exclusive remedy is an intentional tort. An intentional tort shall exist only when an employee is injured as a result of a deliberate act of the employer and the employer specifically intended an injury. An employer shall be deemed to have intended to injure if the employer had actual knowledge that an injury was certain to occur and willfully disregarded that knowledge. The issue of whether an act was an intentional tort shall be a question of law for the court. This subsection shall not enlarge or reduce rights under law.

In *Travis v Dreis & Krump Mfg. Co., 453 Mich 149, 173-74; 551 NW2d 132, 143 (1996)*, the Michigan Supreme Court concluded that the Legislature intended that the plaintiff must demonstrate that a supervisor had actual knowledge that an injury would follow from the deliberate acts or omissions of the employer. In addition, the Michigan Supreme Court concluded that when an injury was "certain" to occur, there was "no doubt" that it would occur. Therefore, the Court held that the laws of probability and scientific proof addressing the odds or percentage of occurrence were insufficient to prove certainty. In addition, the Court held that conclusory statements by experts are insufficient to satisfy the certainty of injury requirement. *Gray v Morley (After Remand), 460 Mich. 738, 742; 596 NW2d 922, 925 (1999)*. In *Agee v. Ford Motor Co., 208 Mich. App. 363, 364; 528 NW2d 768, 769 (1995)*, the Michigan Court of Appeals held that the plaintiffs' intentional tort allegation based on expert testimony concerning the probability of injury was insufficient to circumvent the exclusive remedy provision of the worker's compensation act.

The toxic tort attorney should research the law concerning worker's compensation as the exclusive remedy in the relevant jurisdiction.

CHAPTER NINE

INFORMATION GATHERING AND SELECTED FORMS

I am the very pattern of a modern Major-Gineral,
I've information vegetable, animal, and mineral;
I know the kings of England, and I quote the fights historical,
From Marathon to Waterloo, on order categorical;

Sir William Schwenck Gilbert
The Pirates of Penzance

Information gathering is as important in toxic tort litigation as it is in all areas of litigation. The information gathering process involves the learning of facts about the circumstances of the exposure from clients as well as the review of documents and other sources of information.

The first step in the information gathering process involves the initial client interview. It is important to obtain a history of the exposure event from the client. Clients should be asked to bring to the interview all documentary information that they may have concerning the exposure including material safety data sheets, medical records, and reports that they may have concerning the exposure. Clients should also be asked to bring any photographs or videotapes that they may have concerning the toxin exposure or its consequences. The clients may also know of newspaper articles or news reports concerning the toxin exposure.

It is important that the client complete a questionnaire providing relevant information concerning the toxin exposure. This is particularly important in mass toxic tort cases where completed questionnaires are of great help in processing client responses to interrogatories. The following is a modification of a questionnaire that the author first obtained from Donnelly W. Hadden, Esq. Mr. Hadden, who is a former chairman of the Environmental Law Section of the State Bar of Michigan, was a pioneer in mass environmental and toxic tort litigation in Michigan and has been a mentor of the author.

TOXIC TORT CASE QUESTIONNAIRE

1. Name:
2. Age:
3. Date of Birth:
4. Social Security Number:
5. Spouse's Name:
6. Address:
7. Telephone Numbers (home, work, cellular, and pager):
8. Names, ages and relationship to you of all other people who stay in the home:
9. Do you work? (Yes or No); if "yes" where? Answer for everyone who stays in the house.
10. Is there any dust, fumes, chemicals or bad smells where you work? (Yes or No) If "yes", please describe.
11. Who do you want to complain about?
12. How far do you live from there?
13. What direction do you live from there?
14. Describe the environmental condition(s) you are complaining about.
15. When did you first notice these conditions?
16. Describe when and how often they happen.
17. Have you ever complained to the polluter(s) about these conditions? (Yes or No) If "yes" when, to whom, how (by letter, telephone, other). What did you say and what did they say?
18. Have you ever complained to any governmental agency or official about these conditions? If so, when, to whom, how (by letter, telephone, other). What did you say and what did they say?
19. Have you ever been to any meetings or hearings where the subject of these conditions was discussed? (Yes or No) If "yes", when, where, who called the meeting, who was there, what was decided and what was done.
20. Has anyone ever done any scientific sampling, instrument readings or conducted a study of any kind at or near your home to prove or measure the conditions you complain about? (Yes or No) If "yes", what, when, where, and by whom. Have you ever been given a copy of the results of the work? (Yes or No)
21. Have you ever seen or read any reports, newspaper stories, TV programs or any kind of information about these conditions, and who or what causes them? (Yes or No) If "yes", what, when and where?

22. When was your home built?

23. What is the square footage of your home?

24. Please describe your home (brick or wood, style, number of stories, basement, etc.). Please attach a drawing of the approximate layout of each story of your home. Please also attach front, side and rear photographs of your home.

25. What is the zoning classification where your home is located? (Residential single family, residential multi-family, commercial, industrial, agricultural, other)

26. If you own your home, when did you buy it?

27. What was the purchase price?

28. From whom did you purchase the home?

29. Why did you buy a home in this neighborhood?

30. If you rent, how much is your current monthly rent?

31. Has your rent changed during the last five years?

32. Has your rent changed due to environmental conditions? (Yes or No) If "yes", how much and when?

33. Were you told about any bad environmental conditions before you moved in? (Yes or No) If "yes", what were you told and by whom?

34. Since you have lived in your home, have you made any improvements to the building or the property? (Yes or No) If "yes", list each improvement, the approximate date it was done and how much it cost.

35. Your estimate of the current market values of your home in its present condition.

36. Do you think that your home is worth less than it should be because of the environment? (Yes or No) If "yes", how much do you think it should be worth if there were no environmental problem?

37. Have you ever tried to sell your home? (Yes or No) If "yes", when and for how much money? Were there any offers for you home? (Yes of No) If "yes", how much was offered? Did you have a broker? Please give the name, address and telephone number of the broker.

38. Has your home ever been appraised? (Yes or No) If "yes", when, by whom, and for what reason. What was the appraised value?

39. Have you ever protested your tax evaluation, claiming that your assessment was too high given the environmental conditions? (Yes or No) If "yes", when, to whom, and with what result. If you appealed the decision, to whom did you appeal and with what result?

40. Has the pollution condition caused any physical damage to your home such as discoloration, pitting of painted metal surfaces, corrosion, vibration

cracks, etc.? (Yes or No) If "yes", please list the places or parts damaged and the kind of damage done. Have you made any repairs or done anything to correct the damage or prevent the damage? (Yes or No) If "yes", what, when, and how much did it cost? Do you have any photographs, receipts, estimates or other proof of the damage and what, if anything, you have done about it? (Yes or No) If "yes", list what you have done and provide copies.

41. Has the pollution caused any damage to property other than your home, for example; to cars, lawn furniture, inside furniture, carpets, draperies, plants or animals? (Yes or No) If "yes" please list each item and when and how it was damaged.

42. Were any of these items repaired or corrected? Were steps taken to prevent further damage? (Yes or No) If "yes" state whether you made the repairs or took preventive measures. List the approximate number of hours of labor involved.

43. Do you have any photographs, receipts, estimates or other proofs of the damage and what, if anything, you have done about it?

44. Have you scrapped, thrown away, given away or sold any items that you believe to have been damaged by the pollution condition? (Yes or No) If "yes", list the items, when you got rid of them and why. If any were sold at a loss because of the damage, list the actual sale price and what you feel should have been the proper price without pollution damage.

45. Has the environmental contamination interfered with any business activities that you conduct on your property? (Yes or No) If "yes", list the kind of business and the way that it has been hindered. How much money do you claim that you lost due to interference with business activities due to the environmental conditions? List what proof you have for this loss.

46. Have you or anyone in your household had any actual physical illness or disease which could have been caused by or aggravated by the environmental conditions that you complain about? (Yes or No) If "yes", please list the condition and the name, address, and telephone number of all physicians that have treated these conditions.

47. Do you or anyone in your home suffer from any of the following medical conditions? Please list who suffers from the condition and which physician made the diagnosis:

a.   diabetes;
b.   hypertension (high blood pressure);

c.   heart disease such as cyanosis, angina, heart attack, congestive heart failure, or cardiac arrhythmia;

d.   lung disease such as asthma, emphysema, chronic bronchitis (COPD), emphysema, pulmonary fibrosis or interstitial lung disease (scarring of the lungs), black lung, silicosis, asbestosis, pneumoconiosis, lung cancer, or mesothelioma;

e.   gastrointestinal disease such as liver disease, gastroesophageal reflux disease, gastric or peptic ulcer, Crohn's disease, ulcerative colitis, cancer of the mouth, larynx, esophagus, stomach, pancreas, small bowel, colon, or rectum;

f.   kidney or bladder disease such as kidney failure, blood or pus in the urine, pain on urination, unusual color or smell of the urine, kidney or bladder stones, kidney or bladder cancer;

g.   connective tissue disease such as lupus or scleroderma;

h.   endocrine disease such as thyroid disease, adrenal disease, or pituitary disease;

i.   musculoskeletal disease such as rheumatoid arthritis or osteoarthritis;

j.   disease of the nervous system such as strokes, seizures, loss of consciousness, tumor or cancer of the brain or nervous system; or

k.   psychiatric disease.

48. Do you or anyone in your home suffer from allergies? If "yes", who and to what.

49. List all medications you and anyone in your home are taking. List the name, address and telephone number of the physician that prescribed the medication.

50. List all jobs that you and anyone in your home have held. Include the name, address, and telephone number of your employer and the dates of employment. Describe the nature of each job including work conditions and any chemical or metal exposures.

51. List the smoking, alcohol, and drug history or everyone living in your home.

52. List all pets living in your home.

53. List any "family" diseases such as asthma, heart disease, or cancer that have afflicted more than one member of your family.

54. Please describe any other medical conditions that you believe are related to your toxin exposure.

FREEDOM OF INFORMATION REQUESTS

In addition to information gathered through the client interview and questionnaire, it is often helpful to obtain governmental records concerning the toxin exposure. The following are examples of forms requesting release of governmental information. The first form cites the relevant statute in Michigan. The second form cites the federal statute.

Date:

To:

Re:

> Pursuant to MSA § 4. 1801(1) et seq., I hereby request the following information:

1. The file number or other identification code you have assigned to
2.
3.
4.
5. Copies of such other documents connected with this request as I may designate.

Please call my office when these documents are available so I may decide whether to inspect them at your office prior to copying or not.

I agree to pay all required fees in connection with this request, up to _____ dollars.

Sincerely,

John Doe, Esq.

Date:

To: *United States Environmental Protection Agency*
          Region V
          230 S. Dearborn St.
          Chicago, IL 60604

          Attn: Freedom of Information Officer

Re:

Dear Sir or Madam:

   Pursuant to 5 USC § 552 et seq. and 40 CFR Part 2, I hereby request the following information:

   1.   *The file number or other identification code you have assigned to*
   2.
   3.
   4.
   5.   *Copies of such other documents connected with this request as I may designate.*

Please call my office when these documents are available so I may decide whether to inspect them at your office prior to copying or not.

I agree to pay all required fees in connection with this request, up to _____ dollars

Sincerely,

John Doe, Esq.

THE TOXIC TORT COMPLAINT

Anno domini—that's the most fatal complaint of all in the end.

James Hilton
Goodbye, Mr. Chips

The complaint in a toxic tort action must take into account the elements of the action as well as the damages available to the plaintiff in a toxic tort action. The following is an example of a complaint in a mass toxic tort case where the author was one of the attorneys for the plaintiffs. The case involved a neighborhood where there had been frequent intrusions into basements from combined sanitary and storm sewers. An interesting element in this case was the discovery by the author that the sewage was heavily contaminated with polychlorinated biphenyls (PCBs). In fact, the contamination was so heavy that the testing laboratory was required by federal law to dispose of the samples at a hazardous waste disposal facility. Since the case involved intrusions onto the property of a number of the plaintiffs, the complaint contained elements of a common law suit for trespass-nuisance. The defendant in the complaint was a municipality that owned and controlled the sewers. At the time that the complaint was filed the law in the State of Michigan provided an exemption for governmental immunity in cases involving trespass-nuisance. At that time the law provided for strict liability in the case of sewer intrusions. Since the time that this complaint was filed, the law has changed to require a finding of negligence on the part of the defendant municipality was well as limiting recovery to only economic damages. Although the law has changed, this complaint remains a good example of a complaint in a large mass toxic tort case. The names and other identifiers of the parties have been changed.

The following complaint is presented since it involves a situation that is frequently encountered in mass toxic tort cases. It is common that when toxin contamination involves a residential community, there are a number of classes of plaintiffs with different exposures and damages. In this case there were three classes of plaintiffs. The first class of plaintiffs (Class I) consisted of persons that currently lived in the contaminated area. In additional to personal injury claims, they suffered damage to real property and personal property due to the intrusions of PCB contaminated sewage. The second class of plaintiffs (Class II) consisted of persons that formerly lived in the contaminated area. These persons had personal injury claims as well as claims for damages to personal property due to intrusion of PCB contaminated sewage. The third class of plaintiffs (Class III) consisted of persons who never resided in the contaminated area but had been frequent visitors. These persons commonly were involved in helping residents and friends that lived in the area clean PCB contaminated sewage from their basements. These persons had only personal injury claims. The complaint is interesting since it seeks compensation for economic damages in the form of medical monitoring expenses and increased insurance costs.

STATE OF MICHIGAN
IN THE CIRCUIT COURT FOR
THE COUNTY OF X

Residents of Y Avenue
    Class I (Current Residents)
    Class II (Former Residents)
    Class III (Frequent Visitors)
        Plaintiffs,

v.

CITY OF Z, a Municipal Corporation,
        Defendant.

_____/

COMPLAINT

Plaintiffs, by their attorneys, complain of defendants and declare:

1. Plaintiffs are all present or former residents, occupants or frequent visitors to homes located on Y Avenue, in the City of Z, X County, Michigan. Defendant City of Z is a Municipal Corporation located in X County. These causes of action arose in X County, Michigan. The amount in controversy is in excess of $25,000.

2. Plaintiffs are joined under the provisions of MCR 2.206(A) because their claims arise out of the same occurrences or transactions and there are common questions of fact and law.

3. At all times pertinent, the City of Z was the owner and in possession of underground sewer conduits, pipes or lines which provide sewer service to plaintiffs' homes, former homes, or homes which they often visited.

4. The defendant is and was in control of raw sewage that it accepts into its sewage system.

5. On numerous occasions over more than three years, raw sewage from the city's sewer has physically intruded into the plaintiffs' homes and property. This sewage has and does sometimes contain toxic materials.

6. These intrusions are so noxious and offensive so as to cause a nuisance condition in plaintiffs' homes and property.

7. These sewage intrusions constitute a trespass into the plaintiffs' homes and property.

8. Plaintiffs, due to their exposure to this sewage and its toxic components have an increased risk of contracting serious disease in the future, including cancer.

9. Early diagnosis of the diseases for which the plaintiffs are at increased risk due to their exposure is medically valuable.

10. Protocols of medical monitoring are available to enhance the early detection of disease that plaintiffs are at increased risk of developing due to their exposures as stated above.

11. Plaintiffs will suffer as a proximate result of their increased risk of disease due to the exposures stated above, consequential economic damages in the form of increased insurance premiums for health and life insurance.

12. As a proximate result of the aforesaid trespass-nuisance, plaintiffs in class I have sustained certain injuries and damages, including, but not limited to:

   a. Physical damages to their real property;
   b. Damage and loss of personal property;
   c. Diminution in the value of their property;
   d. Loss of the normal use and enjoyment of their property;
   e. Annoyance, inconvenience and discomfort, including mental stress and emotional anguish;
   f. Impairment of their health;
   g. Reasonable expenses for medical care, treatment and services past, present, and future;
   h. Reasonable and necessary expenses of medical monitoring or surveillance; and
   i. Increased health and life insurance premium costs.

13. As a proximate result of the aforesaid trespass-nuisance, plaintiffs in class II, who formerly resided on Y Avenue, have sustained certain injuries and damages, including, but not limited to:

   a. Damage and loss of personal property;
   b. Loss of normal use and enjoyment of their property;
   c. Annoyance, inconvenience and discomfort, including mental stress and emotional anguish;
   d. Impairment of their health;

e. Reasonable expenses of medical care, treatment and services past, present, and future;

f. Reasonable and necessary expenses of medical monitoring or surveillance; and

g. Increased health and life insurance premium costs.

14. As a proximate result of the aforesaid trespass-nuisance, plaintiffs in class III, who frequently visited residences on Y Avenue, have sustained certain injuries and damages, including, but not limited to:

a. Annoyance, inconvenience and discomfort, including mental stress and emotional anguish;

b. Impairment of their health;

c. Reasonable expenses for medical care, treatment and services, past, present, and future;

d. Reasonable and necessary expenses of medical monitoring or surveillance; and

e. Increased health and life insurance premium costs.

WHEREFORE each plaintiff requests this court to grant him/her judgment against the defendant in such sum in excess of $25,000 to which he/she may be entitled, plus interest from the filing of this complaint, costs and attorney fees.

PART TWO

TECHNICAL ISSUES

This part of the book deals with issues that are not part of the knowledge base of most attorneys. Success in the field of toxic substances litigation is difficult to achieve without some basic knowledge of key concepts and terms. Most attorneys working in this area of law develop a knowledge base sufficient to work effectively. This part of the book will provide, in a simplified format, a primer to the technical issues that underlie many toxic substances cases.

MATHEMATICS

*To myself I seem to have been only like a boy playing on the
sea-shore, and diverting myself in now and then finding a
smoother pebble or a prettier shell than ordinary, whilst the
great ocean of truth lay all undiscovered before me.*

Sir Isaac Newton

It is a general rule of thumb for publishers that the readership of any popular book is decreased by one half for each mathematical formula appearing in the book. There have been a number of recent popular books dealing with mathematical issues that have not contained a single formula. This is understandable since a phobia of mathematics is one of the most common phobias. In many areas of legal practice a lack of mathematical knowledge is of little or no hindrance. However, in toxic substances litigation, a deficiency in mathematics can be a serious handicap. This is not to say that an attorney must be an accomplished mathematician in order to competently handle a toxic substances case. However, many fine points and opportunities for dazzling advocacy will be lost to the attorney who has not developed a basic level of mathematical sophistication. The author has seen a prominent attorney on one occasion become utterly confused at trial because he did not know that 5.6×10^{-6} mg meant 0.0000056 mg.

It is highly advisable that the attorney dealing on a regular basis with toxic substances litigation develop a basic competence in mathematics including algebra, calculus, and statistics.

STATISTICS

A single death is a tragedy, a million deaths is a statistic.

Joseph Stalin

The previous chapter generally warned of the importance of a sophisticated knowledge of mathematics for the serious toxic tort practitioner. Of the disciplines within mathematics, the most important for the practice of toxic tort law is statistics. This brief overview can not begin to provide the reader with the level of competence in statistics needed to be a superb toxic tort litigator. Rather, it is the intent of the author to illustrate a few key advocacy points utilizing basic statistical concepts and a knowledge of the historical origin of the discipline.

Probability

The probability of an event occurring is the chance of the occurrence of that particular event divided by the chance of all possible occurrences. Probability is best demonstrated by games of chance. In fact, the study of probability originated from the fascination of the European upper classes with gambling during the Seventeenth Century.

For example, if one throws a fair die, there is a one sixth chance of getting a one. This is because there are six sides to a cubic die. One of the six sides has a single mark. Therefore, the one will have a random probability of being on top after the die is thrown and settles of one sixth. The probability of throwing a two, three, four, five, or six with a fair die is one sixth for each possible outcome.

The probability of the occurrence of event A occurring is usually denoted as P(A). If there is an event B, the probability of its occurrence is denoted as P(B).

Using our example of the fair die, we can say that getting a one is event A with the probability of getting a one being denoted as P(A). Getting a two is event B with the probability of getting a two being denoted as P(B). The events of getting a three, four, five, or six can be considered events C, D, E, and F with probabilities denoted as P(C), P(D), P(E) and P(F). P(A) through P(F) each have a probability of occurrence of $1/6^{th}$. The sum of all possible occurrences is always 1.

For example, the chance of throwing a one with a single throw of a fair die is P(A) which is 1/6th. The chance of throwing a one or a two with a single throw of a fair die is P(A) + P(B) which is 1/6th plus 1/6th which is equal to 2/6th or 1/3rd. The chance of throwing a one or a two or a three with a single throw of a fair die is P(A) + P(B) + P(C) which is 1/6th plus 1/6th plus 1/6th which is equal to 3/6th or ½. The chance of throwing a one, two, three, four, five, or six with a single throw of a fair die is P(A) + P(B) + P(C) + P(D) + P(E) + P(F) which is 1/6th plus 1/6th plus 1/6th plus 1/6th plus 1/6th plus 1/6th which is equal to 6/6th or 1.

The notation used to indicate the occurrence of event A or event B is P(A U B). The examples of the above throw of the die are mutually exclusive events. You can not throw the die and get a one and a two at the same time.

Therefore, P(A U B) = P(A) + P(B).

If events are not mutually exclusive, there is a chance that events A and B can occur at the same time. The notation used to indicate the occurrence of event A and B is P(A ∩ B).

The probability of the occurrence of non-mutually exclusive events A or B occurring is P(A U B) = P(A) + P(B)—P(A ∩ B).

Events can be dependent or independent. If events are independent, the chance of the occurrence of event A is not made any more or less likely by the occurrence of event B.

For example, say that getting a head on a flip of a fair coin is event H and getting a tail is event T. The probability of event H is P(H) which is equal to ½ and the probability of event T is P(T) which is also equal to ½. Therefore, the probability of getting either a head or a tail on a single flip of a fair coin is P(H) + P(T) which is equal to ½ plus ½ which is 1 since there are only two possibilities. However, say the first flip of the coin produces a head. If the coin is fair, the chance of getting a head or a tail on the second flip is independent of the results of the first flip. The probability of flipping two heads in a row is the probability of getting a head on the first flip times the probability of getting a head on the second flip. Consequently, the probability of flipping two heads in a row is P(H) times P(H) which is ½ times ½ which equals ¼. The probability of flipping two tails in a row is P(T) times P(T) which is ½ times ½ which equals ¼. The probability of flipping a head and a tail in two flips of a coin is slightly more complicated because you can get a head on the first flip and a tail on the second flip or a tail on the first flip and a head on the second flip. You must first calculate the probability of getting a head on the first flip which is ½ times the probability of getting a tail on the second flip which is ½. The product these probabilities equals ¼. You must then calculate the probability of getting a tail on the first flip which is ½ and a head on the second flip which is ½. The product is of these probabilities equals ¼. Therefore, the probability of a head and a tail in the first two flips of a coin is ¼ plus ¼ which is ½. You will note that the probability of getting two heads or two tails or a head and a tail in the first two flips of a coin is ¼ plus ¼ plus ½ which equals 1. The total equals 1 since the combinations cover all the possibilities and there are no other possibilities in two flips of a coin other than two heads, two tails, or one head and one tail.

The legal reader must now be wondering what the point is to the above discussion of probability. How can this be of use to a toxic tort attorney? The gem of an idea is that if two events are independent, then the probability of the occurrence of the two events is the product of the two events. In mathematical notation $P(A \ B) = P(A)P(B)$. For example, you have two clients that live in two separate apartments in the same buildings next to a company alleged to be emitting into the air a chemical that can cause a serious lung disease. Assume that the published medical literature indicates that the serious lung disease only occurs in one in ten thousand persons without a chemical exposure. Client A has this serious lung disease. The probability of this occurring by chance and without the contribution of the toxic chemical is 1/10,000. This may be persuasive of the claim that the toxic chemical from the neighboring factory caused client A's serious lung disease. What if client B also suffers from the same rare lung disease as client A. The probability of A and B suffering from the same rare lung disease by chance without the contribution of the chemical exposure is 1/10,000 times 1/10,000 if the probabilities of A and B getting the disease are independent. The chance of this happening is one in one hundred million. This is extremely supportive of the assertion that the chemical exposure caused the disease in A and B. The mathematical support for the assertion that the chemical caused the lung increases exponentially as the number of clients with the same rare lung disease increases. The defense attorney's goal is to show that while the disease may be rare, the probabilities of occurrence of disease in A and B are not independent. For example, they may be relatives or they may have social activities or hobbies in common.

The above example shows how even a minor understanding of probability theory can lead the intelligent toxic tort attorney to a powerful tool of persuasion.

TOXICOLOGY

*Alcohol, hashish, prussic acid, strychnine, are weak
dilutions: the surest poison is time.*

Emerson
Society and Solitude

T he sixteenth century Swiss physician, Paracelsus, is credited with a famous
maxim: *Nothing is a poison and everything is a poison, it is only a matter of dose.*
This maxim has proved through the ages to be true. Life giving water, if consumed in
large enough quantities, can be a deadly toxin causing death from convulsions arising
from brain swelling. Oxygen necessary for the maintenance of life can cause severe
and irreversible damage to the lungs.

Toxicology is the discipline involved in the study of poisons and their effects
upon living organisms. Since everything in sufficient doses is a poison, all substances
are fairly within the toxicologist's scope of study.

The term "toxicology" is derived from the ancient Greek word for the
"bow" that was used to shoot poisoned arrows. Toxicology studies the effects of
various doses of substances upon living organisms. Usually the subjects of study
are microscopic organisms or animals. Ethical considerations usually prohibit
the use of human subjects in toxicological studies; however, intentional human
exposure does occur in the context of pharmaceutical drug studies. Knowledge
of the adverse consequences of human exposure to substances often arises from
epidemiological studies usually looking at exposed workers or from case studies of
accidental exposures.

A key concept within toxicology is that of the dose response curve. A dose response
curve is usually a sigmoidal or S-shaped curve with the dose of the substance on the
abscissa (x-axis) and the effect upon the ordinate (y-axis). The sigmoidal nature of the
dose response curve reflects the varying susceptibility of members of a population to
various toxins. Some individuals in a population will be highly sensitive to a given
toxin at low doses and will suffer adverse consequences due to their exposure early or
at low concentrations of toxin exposures. Other individuals will be relatively resistant
to the adverse consequences of exposure to a toxin and will only develop symptoms of

disease late in the course of exposure or at high concentrations of toxin exposure. The sigmoidal dose response curve causes the phenomenon of only one or two persons in a large factory population becoming ill from a toxin exposure while the remaining workers remain disease free.

EPIDEMIOLOGY

There are epidemics of nobleness as well as epidemics of disease.

J.A. Froude
Calvinism

E pidemiology is the study of the distribution of various disease states in populations. The term "epidemiology" is derived from the Greek word meaning upon or afflicting the people. Epidemiology historically dealt with the study of epidemics of infectious diseases. However, epidemiology has expanded its grasp to include the study of diseases arising from toxin exposures. The central concept involved in epidemiology is the comparison of the rates of diseases in persons exposed and not exposed to a potential disease-causing agent.

Epidemiological terms often arise in the course of toxic substances litigation. The following is a short glossary of epidemiological terms that commonly arise:

Prevalence:

The number of persons in a population that are currently suffering from disease.

Incidence:

The number of new cases of disease arising in a susceptible population of persons in a given time period.

Relative Risk:

The comparison of the risk of disease in exposed and non-exposed populations.

Odds Ratio:

The ratio of the odds of developing disease in exposed and non-exposed populations.

Attributable Risk:

The rate of disease in exposed persons that can be attributed to the exposure.

Bias:

A factor that will cause a study or analysis to reach the wrong conclusion. There are a number of forms of bias. One famous form of bias is recall bias. An example of when recall bias may arise is the circumstance where mothers are asked if they took a certain medication during their pregnancy. Mothers with children suffering from birth defects are likely to have a better memory of the medications that they took while pregnant than do mothers of children that did not suffer from birth defects. The reason for this is that mothers with children suffering birth defects have frequently thought about what they may have done to cause the birth defect including the taking of medications. Therefore, these mothers are more likely to remember having taken a certain medication than do mothers with normal children who have given prenatal medical usage little or no thought.

Confounder:

A factor that is associated with the cause of a disease, but is not the actual cause. The classic example of confounding was a study looking at ice-cream consumption and homicides. It was found that there is a close correlation between the amount of ice cream sold at a given time and the number of murders. The thought could be that ice-cream consumption causes people to become more agitated and therefore more homicidal because of a sugar rush. However, the more likely explanation is that more ice cream is sold when the weather is hot than when it is cold. During hot weather, people tend to be more agitated. They also tend to be out and about more than in cold weather. Therefore, ice cream consumption is probably a confounder for the true cause of increased homicides. The true cause of the increase in homicides is probably hot weather.

Cohort Studies:

Studies that follow a group of exposed and non-exposed persons without initial disease. At the end of the study, a comparison of the rates of disease in the exposed and non-exposed populations is made.

Case Control Studies:

The level of exposure to a suspected disease-causing agent is compared between persons with the disease and matched controls without the disease.

LUNG DISEASE

My Lungs began to crow like chanticleer,
That fools should be so deep-contemplative,
And I did laugh sans intermission
An hour by his dial

William Shakespeare
As You Like It, II, vii, 30.

The lungs form bellows, with an excellent design, to exchange fresh air rich in oxygen for waste air laden with carbon dioxide. The air enters through the mouth and courses through the larynx into the trachea. From the trachea the course of air branches into the right and left main stem bronchi. The bronchi branch into progressively smaller airways until they meet their terminus in the alveoli. The alveoli are the site of gas exchange where oxygen and carbon dioxide are exchanged across a thin membrane separating the air sacks of the alveoli and the capillaries of the pulmonary blood circulation. Air poor in oxygen and high in carbon dioxide is pumped by the heart in to the lungs. In the alveoli, blood releases carbon dioxide in exchange for oxygen. From the alveoli, blood returns to the heart from which it is pumped to supply the body with necessary oxygen.

Lung disease falls within a spectrum between two main categories. On one end of the spectrum is obstructive lung disease. On the other end of the spectrum is restrictive lung disease.

Obstructive Lung Disease

Obstructive lung disease occurs when the flow of air into and out of the lungs is impeded. This may occur when there is swelling and inflammation of the lining of the airways such as in chronic bronchitis. It may also occur when supporting structures of the lungs are destroyed so that the elastic recoil of the walls of the airways is lost. The airways then collapse upon themselves during expiration, leading to air trapping and hyperinflation of the lungs. This phenomenon occurs in emphysema. Obstructive lung disease also occurs when there is irritation of the lining of the airways, thus causing spasms of the musculature of the airway walls. This results in constriction of the airways blocking airflow into and out of the lungs. This occurs in patients suffering from asthma.

Chronic Bronchitis:

Chronic bronchitis may be caused by occupational and environmental exposures. A frequent cause of chronic bronchitis is cigarette smoking. Long-term cigarette smoking results in swelling and inflammation of the airways with copious sputum production. Occupational and environmental exposures to dusts, such as asbestos, may also cause chronic bronchitis. Chronic bronchitis is defined clinically as a cough that is persistent and is accompanied by sputum production on most days during a three-month period for at least two years. An obstructive pattern may occur on pulmonary function testing (see Pulmonary Function Testing).

Emphysema:

Emphysema occurs when there has been destruction of the walls of the alveoli causing a loss of elastic recoil of the airways. In normal lungs this elastic recoil prevents the airways from collapsing when positive pressures are generated in the chest cavity during expiration. In emphysema, the airways of the lungs collapse during expiration, resulting in air trapping and hyperinflation of the lungs. The most common cause of emphysema is cigarette smoking. However, emphysema may also occur when there is deficiency of alpha$_1$-antitrypsin. Alpha$_1$-antitrypsin deficiency is an autosomal dominant disorder that is the cause of approximately three percent of all cases of emphysema in America. Occupational and environmental exposures may also cause or contribute to the development of emphysema. An obstructive pattern may occur on pulmonary function testing. There may also be a decrease in the diffusing capacity of carbon monoxide (DL$_{CO}$) across the alveolar membrane. This is a reflection of the decreased number of alveoli functioning in the lungs with emphysema. Chest radiographs may show radiolucency of the lungs with attenuation of pulmonary vascular shadows and flattening of the diaphragms.

Asthma:

Asthma occurs when there is inflammation of the airways with hyperreactivity of musculature of the airways. Airway obstruction is usually reversible with inhalation of bronchodilators. Asthma may be viewed as a form of bronchitis. Chest tightness, shortness of breath, wheezing and cough are common presentations of asthma. A host of occupational and environmental exposures may cause asthma. Asthma may present with reversible obstructive findings on pulmonary function studies. A form of asthma occurring with some occupational and environmental exposures is reactive airway dysfunction syndrome.

Reactive Airway Dysfunction Syndrome:

Reactive airway dysfunction syndrome is a clinical entity that was first described in 1985. Reactive airway dysfunction syndrome (RADS) typically occurs after a massive exposure to an irritating fume, mist, or dust. The exposure usually occurs by accident. Persons suffering from RADS will experience asthma like symptoms such as cough, shortness of breath, and chest tightness. These symptoms will often occur when a person with RADS is re-exposed to the inspiration of irritating substances, even in low concentrations. An element of the definition of RADS is that the patient has no history of asthma. If a history of asthma exists in a person with an exposure and symptoms otherwise consistent with the diagnosis of RADS, the diagnosis would more properly be aggravation or exacerbation of pre-existing asthma. This is a distinction that has more legal impact than clinical significance. RADS will frequently present with normal pulmonary function studies. Methacholine challenge is frequently proposed as a means of documenting RADS when pulmonary function studies are normal. Inhalation of methacholine results in spasm of the airways in persons susceptible to airway hyperreactivity such as occurs in persons with RADS. This provides documentation of airway hyperreactivity, helping to confirm the diagnosis of RADS when pulmonary function studies are normal. However, this confirmation comes at the risk of causing respiratory arrest and death. Exposure of a person to the risk of death from a test conducted solely for a medical-legal purpose obviously raises ethical concerns.

Restrictive Lung Disease

Restrictive lung disease occurs when scarring and fibrosis of the lungs develops. This results in small lungs that are stiff and non-compliant. Causes of restrictive lung disease include hypersensitivity pneumonitis, beryllium disease, silicosis, asbestosis, and hard metal disease.

Hypersensitivity Pneumonitis:

Hypersensitivity pneumonitis is a lung disease that results from allergic sensitization to molds and other allergens. This condition occurs when individuals are repeatedly exposed to inhaled allergens. This causes inflammatory reactions in the lungs, and over time this results in fibrosis and scarring of the lungs. The condition is known by a number of names that depend upon the nature of the exposure and the type of material causing hypersensitivity pneumonitis. These names include farmer's lung, mushroom worker's lung, maple bark stripper's disease, bird fancier's lung, and bagassosis.

Beryllium Disease:

Beryllium is a very lightweight metal used in the aerospace, automotive, and dental industries. It results in a disease that is very similar to sarcoidosis. Sarcoidosis is a granulomatous disease of unknown etiology.

Silicosis:

Silicosis is a lung disease caused by the inhalation of crystalline silicon dioxide. The inhalation of crystalline silicon dioxide results in an inflammatory reaction with fibrosis of the lung. The occupations that place persons at risk of silicosis include: foundry work, sandblasting, mining, and manufacture of glass and ceramics.

Asbestosis:

Asbestosis is the development of fibrosis in the lungs following inhalation of asbestos.

Hard Metal Disease:

Hard metal disease is a fibrotic process of the lungs following exposure to hard metals including tungsten and cobalt. Workers at risk include welders and toolmakers.

Pulmonary Function Testing

Pulmonary function tests give the clinician a non-invasive technique to evaluate lung function. Spirometry is the easiest, least expensive and most commonly performed pulmonary function test. Spirometry measures the flow rate and volume of air expired with a maximal effort. The most useful data obtained during spirometry include the forced expiratory volume at one second (FEV_1), forced vital capacity (FVC), and FEV_1/FVC ratio. In obstructive lung disease there is a decrease in the FEV_1. The FVC may be normal or decreased. The FEV_1/FVC ratio is decreased. In restrictive lung disease, the FEV_1 and FVC are reduced but the FEV_1/FVC ratio may be normal or increased.

PART THREE

SPECIFIC TOXINS

This section looks at a number of specific toxins that are likely to be the subject of toxic substances litigation. There is no attempt to provide an extensive review of all the diseases that can be caused by the specific toxins. Rather, the intent is to provide a brief overview of each toxic substance in order to serve as a starting point for further research.

ACROLEIN

There is no odor so bad as that which arises from goodness tainted.

Walden

Economy

Acrolein is an aldehyde that is used as a chemical intermediate in many industrial processes as well as a biocide and as a component in the production of perfumes and colloidal metals. Acrolein is a clear yellow liquid with a strongly disagreeable odor at room temperature. Acrolein can be formed by the combustion of wood and other organic material including cigarettes. The strong odor of acrolein can be detected at trace levels. Low levels of vapors of acrolein are irritating to the eyes and throat. Higher levels of exposure to acrolein are able to cause pulmonary edema and death. Skin exposure to acrolein can cause skin irritation and painful ulcerations. Although animal studies have shown acrolein to be carcinogenic, the International Agency for Research on Cancer (IARC) has classified acrolein as Group 3. This group classification is indicative of their opinion that there is currently inadequate data in humans and animals to classify acrolein as a carcinogen.

ANTIMONY

As a dog returneth to his vomit, so a fool returneth to his folly.

Proverbs 26:11-13

Antimony is a metalloid that is used to create metal alloys as well as a fire retardant in plastic, rubber, textile, paper, and paints. In addition, it is used as an important component in pigments and munitions primers.

Antimony is a common pollutant in urban air arising from combustion of fossil fuels. In water, antimony accumulates in sediments. Due to its location on the periodic table, antimony has many of the same chemical and toxicological properties as arsenic and lead.

Antimony is poorly absorbed from the gastrointestinal tract but is better absorbed through the respiratory tract.

Acute antimony toxicity presents in a manner similar to arsenicals causing vomiting, diarrhea, colic, and a metallic taste. Antimony also causes gastrointestinal and pulmonary irritation and may cause pulmonary edema.

Chronic exposure to antimony may cause dermatitis, eye irritation, and obstructive pulmonary changes. In addition to dermatitis, antimony exposure can cause transient "antimony spots" as well as pustular eruptions in areas of sweating. Increased numbers of spontaneous abortions and menstrual disturbances have been found in women with antimony exposure. Cardiac arrhythmias have also been reported with antimony exposure. Inhalation of antimony by laboratory rats increases their risk of cancer. The International Agency for Research on cancer (IARC) classifies antimony trioxide as a possible carcinogen.

ARSENIC

"Arsenic and Old Lace"

Title of a play by Joseph Kesselring adapted from the cliché "lavender and old lace" used to described highly respectable old ladies.

Arsenic is a heavy metal that has a notorious history as a poison used in homicides. It was not until the development of a chemical detection method in the 19th century that the usage of arsenic by murders became unpopular. It is interesting that there is a heated debate in the historical community concerning the possible use of arsenic by the British to assassinate Napoleon. This arose because of the detection in the mid 20th century of arsenic in hair samples claimed to have been taken from the scalp of Napoleon at the time of his death.

Arsenic may be found in smelting operations as well as in the chemical, pesticide, and pharmaceutical industries. Arsenic may also be found in treated woods.

The symptoms of acute arsenic poisoning include abdominal pain, vomiting, diarrhea, dehydration and shock. Coma, convulsions, and death may follow these symptoms. Chronic arsenic poisoning may cause hyperkeratosis or thickening of the skin of the palms and soles of the feet. Chronic arsenic poisoning may also cause peripheral neuropathy. Arsenic is a carcinogen that has been linked to skin, lung, and gastrointestinal cancers.

A derivative of arsenic is arsine. Arsine is a colorless gas with the odor of garlic. Arsine gas has been associated with death caused by massive intravascular hemolysis of red blood cells.

ASBESTOS

A little fire is quickly trodden out;
Which, being suffered, rivers cannot quench.

William Shakespeare
III Henry VI, IV. viii

Asbestos refers to a group of metallic silicates that have crystallized as long thin particles. Asbestos exists in various forms, which include chrysotile or white asbestos, crocidolite or blue asbestos, and amosite or brown asbestos. Asbestos gained wide spread usage due to its flexibility and fire retardant properties.

The problem with asbestos is that its thin long fibers are easily inhaled into the lungs. Once the fibers become inhaled, they become trapped in the lungs causing disease. Asbestos exposure can cause asbestosis. Asbestosis is a restrictive lung disease arising from the ability of the asbestos fibers to scar the lungs. Asbestos exposure may also cause a cancer of the lining of the lungs called mesothelioma. In addition, asbestos exposure may also cause lung cancer. The risk of lung cancer in asbestos exposed persons is greatly increased by cigarette smoking.

BARIUM

Ice and iron cannot be welded.

Robert Louis Stevenson
Weir of Hermiston

Barium is a silver-white metal that naturally occurs as barite ($BaSO_4$) and as witherite ($BaCO_3$). These compounds are relatively insoluble. Barium sulfide, barium chloride, and barium hydroxide are water soluble.

Barium is used in the petroleum industry as a drill lubricant, as a white pigment in paint, as filler for paper, as a component of saltwater-resistant cement, as a rodenticide, and as a flux for welding rods. In addition, barium sulfate is used commonly as a radiographic contrast medium.

The water soluble barium salts are strongly alkaline and may cause eye, nose, throat, and respiratory tract irritation. Intoxication with the soluble salts stimulates contraction of smooth, cardiac, and striated muscles. Poisoning victims may present with vomiting, abdominal pain, tachycardia, shortness of breath, cyanosis, and muscular paralysis. Electrocardiographic abnormalities have also been noted. Welders using welding rods with barium flux have been found to have elevated plasma barium levels.

Barium sulfate is highly insoluble in water. This property renders it safe for use as a radiographic contrast material for oral ingestion. However, inhalation of barium sulfate may cause a benign pneumoconiosis known as baritosis. Baritosis presents as small, well defined, radiographic densities throughout the chest on X-rays; however, pulmonary function is not impaired.

BENZENE

B enzene is a volatile, colorless, clear flammable liquid that has been used as a solvent in adhesives and paint removers. Benzene has also been used in the synthesis of plastics and explosives.

Benzene is absorbed by inhalation as well as through the skin. The acute symptoms of benzene intoxication include fatigue, headache, nausea, narcosis, and loss of consciousness. Acute benzene intoxication may cause death. The chronic consequences of benzene exposure include aplastic anemia and leukemia. Benzene has also been suspected of causing multiple myeloma.

BERYLLIUM

*Sickness is the mother of modesty, putteth us in mind of our
mortality; and when we are in the full career of worldly pomp and
jollity, she pulleth us by the ear, and maketh us know ourselves.*

Robert Burton
The Anatomy of Melancholy II. 3.2

B eryllium is an extremely lightweight but strong metal that is frequently used in the
aerospace industry. Acute effects of beryllium exposure include nasopharyngitis,
tracheobronchitis, and pneumonitis. Implantation of beryllium under the skin can
cause formation of non-caseating granulomas. Chronic beryllium disease presents
as pulmonary granulomas. Chronic beryllium disease can be easily confused with
sarcoidosis. The International Agency for Research on Cancer has classified beryllium
as a carcinogen.

CADMIUM

The mind is seldom quickened to very vigorous operations
but by pain, or the dread of pain. We do not disturb ourselves
with the detection of fallacies which do us no harm.

Samuel Johnson
The Idler No. 18

Cadmium is a heavy metal that is recovered as a by-product of the smelting of zinc ores. Cadmium is also recovered during the smelting of some lead ores. Cadmium is used in electroplating as well as in the formation of pigments. Cadmium is also used as a stabilizer in plastics as well as a component in nickel cadmium batteries. The presence of cadmium as a pigment is one of the reasons why illustrated magazines should never be burned as a fuel in home fireplaces or grills. The burning forms a cadmium rich ash that is bio-available through inhalation. Prior to the discovery of its harmful effects, cadmium was used to plate the interiors of tin cans holding food products.

Chronic cadmium poisoning causes calcium losing kidney damage, which can result in hypertension. The urinary calcium loss with cadmium intoxication causes a form of severe osteoporosis called itai-itai disease. Itai-itai is Japanese for ouch-ouch. The disease was first diagnosed in Japanese women working in rice paddy fields contaminated with cadmium from munitions factories during World War II. The women developed pathologic bone fractures with minor trauma.

There is evidence that cadmium workers have a higher than expected incidence of lung and prostate cancer.

CARBON MONOXIDE

*There can no great smoke arise, but there must be some
fire, no great report without great suspicion.*

John Lyly
Euphues

Carbon monoxide is a colorless and odorless gas that most commonly occurs due to the incomplete combustion of fossil fuels. Carbon monoxide binds tightly to hemoglobin, thus preventing proper oxygenation of the tissues of the body. Carbon monoxide intoxication can cause brain damage and death.

Methylene chloride is metabolized within the body to form carbon monoxide. Methylene chloride used in furniture stripping can cause fatal carbon monoxide poisoning.

An interesting aspect of carbon monoxide poisoning is that some poisoning victims develop cherry red skin.

CARBON TETRACHLORIDE

Cleanliness is indeed, next to godliness.

John Wesley

Carbon tetrachloride is a halogenated hydrocarbon that was used in dry cleaning, degreasing operations, fumigation, as well as in fire extinguishers. The Occupational Safety and Health Administration (OSHA) has classified carbon tetrachloride as a carcinogen.

The adverse health effects of carbon tetrachloride include liver and kidney toxicity. Carbon tetrachloride is also a central nervous system depressant causing dizziness, blurred vision, headache, lethargy, and coma.

CHLOROFORM

To die, to sleep, no more; and by asleep to say we end the heartache,
and the thousand natural shocks that flesh is heir to.
Tis a consumation devoutly to be wish'd.
To die, to sleep. To sleep, perchance to dream: ay, there's the
rub! For in that sleep of death what dreams may come. When
we have shuffled off this mortal coil, must give us pause.

William Shakespeare
Hamlet III.i.

Chloroform is a halogenated hydrocarbon also known as trichloromethane. Chloroform was once used as an anesthetic for surgery. OSHA and the National Institute for Occupational Safety and Health (NIOSH) both classify chloroform as a carcinogen. The International Agency for Research on Cancer (IARC) classifies chloroform as a Group 2B compound, indicating that it is possibly carcinogenic to humans.

Acute exposure to chloroform causes dryness of the mouth, thirst, lethargy, lightheadedness, gastrointestinal discomfort and urinary frequency. Cardiac arrhythmias have also been reported.

CHROMATED COPPER ARSENATE (CCA)

If the tree fall towards the south, or toward the north, in
the place where the tree falleth, there it shall be.

Ecclesiastes 11:3

Chromated copper arsenate is a compound that has been used to pressure-treat wood in order to make the wood resistant to rot and insect damage. The problem with pressure treated wood is the ability of CCA to leach out of the wood. This causes human and animal exposure to the harmful components of CCA with particular concern being exposure to arsenate. Exposure also occurs with generation of sawdust in cutting and with formation of ash during burning of CCA-treated wood. CCA-treated wood is commonly used for outside fixtures such as decks. The lifetime of CCA-treated wood is approximately thirty years. Since the use of CCA-treated wood became very popular in the 1960s and 1970s; there is growing concern about ground water contamination with CCA as a result of disposal of treated wood products in unlined landfills.

Compounds containing arsenic are known for their toxicological and carcinogenic properties (see ARSENIC).

CHROMIUM

C hromium is a metal that is used as a pigment and as a metal plating agent. Chromium is irritating and exposure to chromic acid is known to cause nasal irritation and septal perforation in chrome-plating workers. Contact dermatitis is a common reaction to chrome exposure.

The Environmental Protection Agency (EPA) and IARC have concluded that hexavalent chromium is a human carcinogen.

COBALT

Man is a tool-using animal. Nowhere do you find him without tools;
without tools he is nothing, with tools he is all.

Thomas Carlyle
Sartor Resartus I

C obalt is a silvery gray to black metal that is most frequently used as a component of hard metal cutting tools. Cobalt is also used as a pigment in glass, china, and paint.

Cobalt exposure through inhalation causes respiratory illness that is termed "hard metal disease." Individuals who have inhaled cobalt can suffer from asthma as well as from restrictive pulmonary disease. Cobalt was used in the 1960's as an agent to improve the foaming characteristics of beer. This usage led to the discovery that cobalt can cause cardiomyopathy.

CYANIDE

Cyanide is a toxin that arises in a number of industrial settings. Cyanide also occurs naturally in a number of plants including fruits and vegetables. Fatal poisoning can result from cyanide released in fires.

Cyanide acts as a poison of cellular respiration with a fast onset of action. Hydrogen cyanide is used as a pesticide and as a fumigant. Cyanide was the agent used in the suicides of Hermann Goering, Heinrich Himmler, Eva Braun, and Adolph Hitler.

DIBROMOCHLOROPROPANE

I, the heir of all ages, in the foremost files of time.

Tennyson
Locksley Hall

Dibromochloropropane is a nematocide that is known to cause male infertility. Workers that were exposed to dibromochloropropane during its manufacture were shown to suffer from testicular changes that were dependent upon the duration of occupational exposure. Azoospermia (absence of living sperm in semen) as well as oligospermia (low sperm count in semen) have been found in exposed workers. Decreased fertility and hormonal abnormalities have persisted in some workers after cessation of exposure.

DICHLORODIPHENYLTRICHLOROETHANE (DDT)

Thou shalt not nede to be afrayed for any bugges by night.

Psalms 91:5

Dichlorodiphenyltrichloroethane (DDT) is an organochloride insecticide that is banned in the United States. Beginning in the 1940's, organochloride insecticides were in widespread use in agriculture as well as in malaria and lice control programs. DDT accumulates in body fat and tends to bioconcentrate through the food chain.

Acute intoxication with DDT causes central nervous system stimulation with paresthesia (abnormal sensation such as burning, pricking, tingling, or tickling) of the tongue, face, and lips as well as of the extremities in severe cases of intoxication.

2,3,7,8-TETRACHLORODIBENZO-P-DIOXIN (DIOXIN)

He jests at scars that never felt a wound.

William Shakespeare
Romeo and Juliet II. ii.

D ioxin is a by-product of some processes of chemical synthesis. Dioxin is also known as TCDD. Dioxin may be absorbed through inhalation as well as through ingestion and dermal contact. Dioxin is known to cause severe chloracne. Chloracne or tar acne is an acne-like skin eruption that is caused by exposure to certain chlorinated chemical compounds.

NIOSH has classified dioxin as an occupational carcinogen. The EPA and IARC have classified dioxin as a probable human carcinogen.

FORMALDEHYDE

The Egyptian mummies, which Cambyses or time hath spared, avarice now consumeth. Mummy is become merchandise, Mizraim cures wounds, and pharaoh is sold for balsams.

Sir Thomas Browne
Of Ambition and Fame

Formaldehyde is widely used in industrial settings and is commonly found in the environment. Formaldehyde is used in many commercial products such as in particleboard, furniture, plastics, rubbers, and textiles. Formaldehyde can be released in a gaseous state from these products, thus leading to human exposure in homes, offices, and schools. The medical and mortuary professions use formaldehyde as an embalming agent and as a tissue preservative.

Formaldehyde is irritating to the eyes, mucous membranes and lungs.

LEAD

Lead is a heavy metal that has been used since antiquity. One theory holds that one of the factors leading to the fall of the Roman Empire was the use of lead pipes to supply water to the upper classes.

Lead acts as a poison of vital enzymes within the body. Lead is a poison affecting the kidneys, nervous system, reproductive system, as well as the hematopoietic (blood-forming) system. Lead dust and fumes are well absorbed by the respiratory system.

While adults can suffer damage to the nervous system due to lead intoxication, the nervous systems of developing children are extremely sensitive to the harmful consequences of lead exposure.

Damage to the kidneys by lead can cause hypertension in both adults and children.

Lead intoxication can result in male infertility. This is of concern since lead-intoxicated females can be fertile resulting in devastating congenital lead intoxication in the unborn child. The tragedy of insemination by a sperm donor in a case where both a husband and wife are lead intoxicated is obvious. Since lead dust can be easily transported home on the clothing of workers, the possibility of a husband and wife both being lead intoxicated due to an occupational exposure is not remote.

Lead intoxication can result in anemia that can be easily overlooked or misdiagnosed as anemia due to iron deficiency.

MANGANESE

It has taken a great deal of energy, which has not been so difficult to
summon as the necessary patience to wait, simply wait much of the
time until my instincts assured me that I had assembled my materials
in proper order for a final welding into their natural form.

Hart Crane

M anganese is a silvery white metal that was used in the oxide form by the ancient Greeks in the manufacture of glass. Manganese is used primarily in the metallurgical industry; however, welding rods and fluxes also contain manganese. Manganese is irritating to the eyes, skin and mucous membranes. However, the most serious consequence of manganese poisoning is a condition that resembles Parkinson's disease. Although the ability of manganese to cause a condition resembling Parkinson's disease was first described in 1837; development of "manganism" in workers exposed to welding fumes has recently become an area of concern.

MERCURY

As with my hat upon my head
I walk's along the Strand,
I there did meet another man
With his hat in his hand

Samuel Johnson

Mercury is a metal that is liquid at room temperature. Intoxication usually results from inhalation of mercury vapors in the case of elemental mercury or from oral ingestion in the case of inorganic and organic mercury.

The earliest findings of mercury intoxication are gingivitis (inflammation of the gums), hypersalivation and a bitter metallic taste in the mouth. The classic symptoms of mercury intoxication include shyness, tremor, irritability, and psychosis. Mercury intoxication can also result in kidney damage with a resulting generalized swelling of the body.

Poisoning with organic mercury can result in devastating damage to the central nervous system such as occurred in Minamata Bay, Japan, due to consumption of contaminated seafood.

Mercury intoxication received attention during the adventures of Alice in Wonderland. The term "Mad Hatter" was a reference to mercury toxicity. In Victorian England, mercury was used in the production of hats. Mercury toxicity in workers manufacturing hats caused the term "mad as a hatter" to become a common expression.

Early scientists were frequently exposed to mercury vapors with insanity occurring due to mercury toxicity. The expression that one is a "mad scientist" arose due to the common occurrence of mercury toxicity in early researchers.

MOLDS

The woods decay, the woods decay and fall,
The vapours weep their burthen to the ground,
Man comes and tills the field and lies beneath,
And after many a summer dies the swan.

Tennyson
Tithonus

Pathogenic fungi, such as stachybotrys, are able to cause injury to humans through allergic reactions and toxic metabolites. The dangers of mycotoxins are demonstrated by their possible use as chemical warfare agents used in Southeast Asia and Afghanistan. Aspergillus forms a mycotoxin that is recognized by the International Agency for Research on Cancer (IARC) as being a human carcinogen. Exposure to pathogenic indoor mold is also linked to the development of respiratory disease such as asthma and interstitial lung disease. The peer-reviewed medical literature also supports a causal connection between prolonged and intense exposure to stachybotrys and the development of disorders of the central nervous system.

OSMIUM

After fingerprints, I went upstairs with this new detective.
And I never saw the other detective again.

O smium is an extremely dense metal that is bluish white in color. It is three times as heavy as iron. When combined with iridium, osmium forms a very hard alloy which is used in the tips of fountain pens. Aqueous solutions of osmium tetroxide where once used for taking fingerprints. However, this practice was discontinued once it was realized that osmium tetroxide caused dermatitis. When osmium powder is allowed to oxidize in air, osmic acid is formed which is extremely irritating to the mucous membranes. Chronic exposure to osmic acid can cause corneal ulceration.

PHOSPHORUS

Without phosphorus there would be no thoughts.

Friedrick Karl Christian Ludwig Büchner

Phosphorus is a metal that was first discovered in human urine by Hennig Brandt in 1674. The three allotropes of phosphorus are white phosphorus, red phosphorus, and black phosphorus. The white (or yellow) allotrope is by far the most toxic.

Phosphorus and its compounds have many uses in modern industry including in the manufacture of explosives, fertilizers, detergents, and insecticides. The historical use of white phosphorus in the manufacture of matches caused an epidemic of "phossy jaw". Workers, usually young women, who were exposed to white phosphorus, developed a painful and disfiguring condition where their jaws would rot away.

PLATINUM

I shoot the Hippopotamus with bullets made of platinum,
because if I use the leaden one his hide is sure to flatten em.

Hilaire Belloc

Platinum is a silver-white metal that was first discovered by the Spaniards about 1735 in Colombia. The term "platina" arises from the Spanish word for silver. The metal is extremely malleable and ductile and is used widely in industry. Platinum is found in many alloys with gold, copper, iridium, cobalt, rhodium, and ruthenium. Platinum is extensively used as a catalyst including in catalytic converters for automobile exhaust systems. Exposure to the salts of platinum can cause allergic phenomena occurring in the nasal mucosa, bronchi and skin which are referred to as "platinosis".

POLYCHLORINATED BIPHENYLS (PCBS)

My skin hangs about me like an old lady's loose gown!
I am withered like an old apple-john.

William Shakespeare
I Henry IV III. iii.

Polychlorinated biphenyls gained widespread use due to their low flammability and electrical properties. They were widely used as insulating materials in transformers.

PCBs are associated with chloracne and toxicity of the liver, kidney and nervous system.

Concerns about the harmful consequences of PCB exposure led to the banning of the manufacture and sale of PCBs in the United States in the late 1970s.

RADIUM

The intense atom glows
A moment, then is quenched in a most cold repose.

Percy Bysshe Shelley
Adonais

R adium was the first radioactive material that was found to be a carcinogen. Radium was tragically used to form a luminous paint for watch dials. Radioactive alpha particles emitted from radium caused crystals in luminous paint to glow.

In the early twentieth century young women were employed to paint radium containing luminous paint onto watch dials. The women were encouraged to form a point on the tip of their brushes with their lips. They would swallow small amounts of radium every time they pointed their brush. These women later suffered degeneration of their jawbones and development of cancers of the bones.

RADON

A blind, fortuitous concourse of atoms.

John Locke

Radon is a gas formed by the decay of radium occurring naturally in the ground. Radon is radioactive and has a half-life of 3.8 days. Radon decays further into "radon daughters" that attach to dust particles in the air. When these dust particles are inhaled, they are deposited in the lungs causing an increased risk of lung cancer due to the radiation exposure.

Underground miners have an increased risk of lung cancer due to radon exposure. Miners in the Carpathian Mountain region of Europe have been known for centuries to suffer from an increased incidence of lung cancer. However, the relationship between their lung cancer and exposure to radon was only recognized in the 1920's. In a study investigating an unexpectedly high incidence of lung cancer in Chinese tin miners, radon exposure was found to be a contributing factor. Uranium miners in the United States and Canada have also been found to suffer from an increased incidence of lung cancer.

Radon gas can accumulate in basements of homes causing an increased risk of lung cancer in the occupants. This is a serious problem since radon gas is colorless and odorless. Consequently, home occupants are usually unaware of their radon exposure.

SILICA

How small are grains of sand! Yet if enough are placed in a ship they sink it.

St. Augustine
Confessions

S ilica or silicon dioxide has been known to cause pulmonary disease since the sixteenth century. Silica inhalation can cause serious lung disease known as silicosis. Silicosis is a restrictive lung disease resulting in scarred and stiff lungs. Pulmonary function testing often shows decreased lung volumes with an increase in the percentage of air exhaled in the first second (FEV 1). Chest X-rays can show increased interstitial lung markings with punctuate densities in the upper lung field.

Persons with silicosis have an increased risk of developing pulmonary tuberculosis.

Acute severe silica exposure can cause rapidly progressive disease leading to death.

VANADIUM

Vanadium is a metal found in crude oil. Workers cleaning boilers can be exposed to high levels of vanadium. Vanadium exposure causes irritation and inflammation of the eyes and respiratory tract.

An interesting manifestation of vanadium toxicity is its ability to turn the tongue green. The coloration of the tongue is due to a chemical coating. The appearance is a greenish discoloration that is similar in appearance to the color of a leaf.

Vanadium is cleared very rapidly from the blood into the urine. Consequently, blood testing is highly likely to product false negative results as to exposure.

PART FOUR

CASE STUDIES

In this final part of the book, six case studies will be presented. Each demonstrate an expert evaluation, with supporting cites from the peer-reviewed medical literature. Three of the cases support the allegations of plaintiffs, while the other three reports support defendants. Three of the reports involve exposure to chemical toxins. One of the reports concerns exposure to a radioactive substance. Another case report concerns an alleged exposure to an infectious agent. The final case report concerns an allegation of injury from an environmental hazard in the form of lightning.

CASE ONE

LUNG CANCER, ASBESTOS EXPOSURE AND CIGARETTE SMOKING

M r. W was a 63-year-old gentleman who died due to complications arising from a bronchogenic carcinoma of the lungs, with massive mediastinal lymphadenopathy, along with complications of superior vena cava syndrome. Mr. W was employed as a foundry worker since 1984. In November of 1996, Mr. W was diagnosed with lung cancer. He died on December 7, 1996, from complications of his lung cancer. There is evidence that Mr. W was exposed to asbestos during the course of his employment. While Mr. W had been a cigarette smoker, he quit smoking in 1977. Prior to 1977 he smoked one pack of cigarettes each day for approximately 25 years.

The issue is whether or not Mr. W's lung cancer was caused or aggravated by his exposure to asbestos which occurred during his employment as a foundry worker. Although Mr. W has a history of being a cigarette smoker, it is significant that he quit smoking twenty years prior to his diagnosis of lung cancer.

It is well known that cigarette smoking causes an increased risk of death from lung cancer. Cigarette smokers have a slightly greater than ten fold increased risk of death from lung cancer as compared to non-smokers. However, this risk gradually decreases after smoking cessation. Twenty years after smoking cessation, there is only a 2.10 fold increased risk of death from lung cancer in previously smoking individuals as compared to persons that have never smoked (*Maxcy-Rosenau-Last, Public Health & Preventive Medicine. 13th edition. Appleton & Lange.* pp. 720-21).

However, in addition to causing an increased risk of asbestosis and mesothelioma, exposure to asbestos causes an increased risk of death from lung cancer. Age-standardized rates of lung cancer deaths per 100,000 person-years showed that individuals who neither smoked, nor worked with asbestos, had a death rate from lung cancer of 11.3 deaths/100,000 person-years. Asbestos workers who did not smoke had a death rate from lung cancer of 58.4 deaths/100,000 person-years. Smokers who were not asbestos workers had a death rate from lung cancer of 122.6 death/100,000 person-years.

However, smokers who were exposed to asbestos had a death rate from lung cancer of 601.6 deaths/100,000 person years *(Maxcy-Rosenau-Last, Public Health & Preventive Medicine. 13th edition. Appleton & Lange. page 344)*. Therefore, asbestos workers who smoke have an increased lung cancer death rate of approximately ten fold greater than asbestos workers who do not smoke. It is believed that the reason for this increased rate of death from lung cancer in smoking asbestos workers, is that carcinogenic materials from cigarette smoke adheres to the surface of asbestos fibers in the lung. This results in a persistent nidus of exposure to carcinogenic materials in the lung with a resulting increased risk of lung cancer.

In this case, two things must be determined. What was Mr. W's risk of death from lung cancer due to his history of cigarette smoking; and what was his risk of lung cancer death due to his history of exposure to asbestos? His risk of death from lung cancer attributable to asbestos exposure can then be determined.

As indicated above, a person who has never smoked and has never been an asbestos worker, has a rate of death from lung cancer of 11.3 deaths/100,000 person-years. However, Mr. W had a risk of death from lung cancer 2.10 times that of a non-smoker due to his history of cigarette smoking cessation 20 years before his death. Persons that stopped smoking 20 years previously have a rate of death from lung cancer of 23.7 deaths/100,000 person-years. However, persons that smoke and are exposed to asbestos have a rate of death from lung cancer of 601.6 deaths/100,000 person-years.

Consequently, the risk of death from lung cancer, attributable to asbestos exposure, in a person who stopped smoking cigarettes twenty years previously is 577.9 deaths/100,000 person-years. Therefore, an asbestos worker who stopped smoking twenty years previously has a greater than twenty four fold increased risk of death from lung cancer as compared to a non-asbestos worker who stopped smoking fifteen years previously. As a result of his exposure to asbestos, Mr. W's risk of death from lung cancer was twenty four times greater than if he had not been exposed to asbestos. In other words, Mr. W had a 2,400-percent increased risk of developing lung cancer, due to his asbestos exposure, as opposed to another person who quit smoking twenty years ago, but was not exposed to asbestos.

PULMONARY FIBROSIS, METAL DUST, AND CIGARETTE SMOKING

M rs. X is a 46-year-old female who was employed at a metal fabrication facility. In 1996, she became a machine operator. Most of the equipment she operated was computerized. The welding area was adjacent to her work area; however, welding activities only occurred for two and one half-hours during her shift. Mrs. X began smoking cigarettes in approximately 1975, and quit smoking in 1999. She also has suffered joint pain and there is mention of her having been diagnosed as suffering from sero-negative rheumatoid arthritis. In 2000, she was diagnosed as suffering from idiopathic pulmonary fibrosis.

The peer-reviewed medical literature provides interesting insights in this matter. Metal dust exposure causes an 11% increased risk of idiopathic pulmonary fibrosis. A history of having ever smoked cigarettes causes a 60% increased risk of idiopathic pulmonary fibrosis. Smokers with a 21 to 40 pack-years history of cigarette smoking have a 130% increased risk of pulmonary fibrosis *(Murray JF, Nadel JA. Textbook of Respiratory Medicine. Third Edition. W.B. Saunders Company. © 2000. Page 1677).* However, persons that have stopped smoking within 2.5 years have a 250% increased risk of developing idiopathic pulmonary fibrosis *(Baumgartner KB, Samet JM, Stidley CA, Colby TV, Waldron JA. Cigarette smoking: a risk factor for idiopathic pulmonary fibrosis. Am J Respir Crit Care Med 1997 Jan; 155 (1):242-8).*

It should also be noted that smoking is a risk factor for the development of overt pulmonary fibrosis in rheumatoid arthritis *(Murray JF, Nadel JA. Textbook of Respiratory Medicine. Third Edition. W.B. Saunders Company. © 2000. Page 1698. Hyland RH, Gordon DA, Broder I, et al: A systemic controlled study of pulmonary abnormalities in rheumatoid arthritis. J Rheumatol 10:395-405, 1983).*

If Mrs. X had a significant exposure to metal dust, she would have an 11% increased risk of developing idiopathic pulmonary fibrosis compared to a similar individual without a history of metal dust exposure. However, as a person who had recently quit smoking, she had a 250% increased risk of developing idiopathic pulmonary fibrosis compared to a similar person who has never been a cigarette smoker. Therefore, even if it is assumed that Mrs. X had a significant exposure to metal dust in her workplace, she would still have more than a 22 times greater risk of developing idiopathic pulmonary fibrosis due to her history of having recently quit a long term cigarette smoking habit.

It should also be noted that it appears likely that Mrs. X is suffering from sero-negative rheumatoid arthritis. Smoking is a risk factor for developing overt idiopathic pulmonary fibrosis in persons with rheumatoid arthritis.

CHEMICAL INDUCED LUNG DISEASE

M s. Y is a 42-year-old woman who occupied a rental villa with another woman while attending a charity function. Ms. Y had one of the bedrooms of the villa, while the other woman occupied another bedroom in the villa.

When Ms. Y first entered into her bedroom in the villa, she noticed a strong chemical smell that she described as being similar to the smell of a new carpet. She noticed a burning sensation of the skin around her nose as well as of the nasal mucosa. At that time, she only stayed in the room briefly to change her clothing before leaving to attend the reception for the charity function. When she returned to the villa for the evening, the other woman staying in the villa remarked that there was a chemical odor coming from the bedroom of Ms. Y.

That evening Ms. Y was not able to fall asleep and stayed up to read in her room. While in the bedroom, she noticed a burning sensation of her eyes and nose. She also experienced difficulty breathing that developed over approximately one hour. She looked into the mirror of her bathroom and noticed that her face was swollen and that her eyes had a reddish appearance. She became alarmed and woke her friend staying in the other bedroom of the villa. Her friend brought her to an emergency department. Ms. Y indicated that the emergency physician was concerned that she had suffered a chemical exposure. He treated her with Benadryl® and steroid injections. She was also given a methylprednisolone dose-pak. She then returned to the villa with her friend. When Ms. Y returned to the villa, she was tired. She did not return to sleep in her own bedroom; rather, she stayed in the room of her friend. Her friend stayed up most of the night checking upon her condition. The next morning she checked out of the villa and returned to her home. Her eyes continued burning after returning home. She saw her optometrist who prescribed eye drops for her. She also noticed the development of symptoms of headache and nasal congestion. She also suffered from facial swelling and redness. She indicated that these problems occurred with exposure to smoke, perfume, cologne, and cleaning materials. She indicated that with these exposures, she feels a sensation like a flame going up her nose with accompanying pressure in her face. She has subsequently learned from the local health department that methylene chloride was used to clean the area of the water-heater in her bedroom in the villa.

A physician at a local hospital diagnosed Ms. Y as suffering from reactive airway dysfunction syndrome. Ms. Y went to an internationally famous university hospital for a second opinion. She indicated that the physicians at the internationally famous university hospital agreed that she was suffering from reactive airway dysfunction syndrome.

She continues to suffer from symptoms of shortness of breath, nasal congestion, and headache with exposure to irritating chemicals, perfumes, and smoke. Her past medical history was negative for diabetes mellitus, hypertension, heart disease, lung disease, asthma, gastrointestinal disease, renal disease, endocrine disease, or musculoskeletal disease other than bursitis. She had no history of disease of the nervous system other than a history of seizures. She had no history of significant headaches prior to the chemical exposure.

Her medications included Claritin®, Duravent®, Prevacid®, Ultram®, and Imitrex®.

She indicated that she has no known allergies. Skin testing at a local hospital showed allergies to cats and dogs. She indicated that she has had dogs all of her life without problems.

She does drink white wine but does not smoke.

Ms. Y's mother suffered a myocardial infarction at the age of 51. Her father died due to cancer with metastases to the brain at the age of 63. The primary site of the cancer was not known. She has two sisters and one brother who are in good health. One sister has allergies to cashew nuts and seafood.

Her review of systems was negative other than bursitis of the shoulders.

Physical examination showed vital signs to be stable with blood pressure of 140/80 and pulse of 62. Pupils were equal, round and reactive to light. Neck was supple without bruits or masses. Lungs were clear to auscultation and percussion. Heart had a regular rate and rhythm without murmur or gallop. Abdomen had positive bowel sounds in all four quadrants. There was no abdominal tenderness to palpation and no palpable organomegaly. Extremities were without edema or cyanosis. Examination of the nervous system showed her to be alert and orientated. Cranial nerves II through XII were intact and there were no gross motor deficits.

Pulmonary function studies were FVC 3.84 liters (116% predicted), FEV1 3.47 liters (125% predicted), %FEV1 90.36% (108% predicted).

Reactive Airways Dysfunction Syndrome (RADS) was first described as a clinical entity in 1985 as a reactive asthma occurring after pulmonary exposure to an irritant. After exposure to a pulmonary irritant, the individual with RADS presents with asthma-like symptoms upon further exposure to irritant fumes *(Rom, W. N., Environmental and Occupational Medicine, Second Edition. 1992. Little, Brown and Company. Page 412. Brooks SM, Weiss MA, Bernstein IL. Reactive airways dysfunction syndrome: Persistent asthma syndrome after high-level irritant exposure. Chest.1985;88:376-384)*. It is common for individuals with RADS to be unable to tolerate cigarette smoke and fumes from household cleaners and perfumes.

Ms. Y will suffer from RADS for an indeterminate period of time. In a study of seven men and three women who developed RADS after exposure to irritant fumes, one person's disease was documented to have persisted at least 12 years after exposure *(Brooks SM, Weiss MA, Bernstein Il. Reactive airway dysfunction syndrome: Persistent asthma syndrome after high-level irritant exposure. Chest. 1985; 88:376-384. Rom WN, Environmental and Occupational Medicine. Page 413)*.

The cause of Ms. Y's RADS, was exposure to methylene chloride vapors as well as probable exposure to phosgene gas. Phosgene gas, which was used as a poison gas during World War I, is known to be produced when methylene chloride is exposed to flame and hot metal *(Raffle P.A.B., Adams P.H., Baxter P.J., Lee W.R. Hunter's Diseases of Occupations 8th edition. Page 147)*. The use of methylene chloride to clean around the water-heater in her bedroom in the villa makes the generation and presence of phosgene likely. Pulmonary toxicity following exposure to methylene chloride and its combustion product phosgene has been reported in the peer reviewed medical literature *(Snyder RW, Mishel HS, Christensen GC. Pulmonary toxicity following exposure to methylene chloride and its combustion product, phosgene. Chest 1992 Mar;101(3):860-1)*.

Methacholine challenge has been used as a diagnostic study concerning RADS in cases where the pulmonary function studies were normal. However, there is a risk of precipitating an acute respiratory arrest with methacholine challenge *(Morris JF, Koski WA, Johnson LC. Spirometric standards for healthy nonsmoking adults. Am Rev Resp Dis. Jan 1971; 103:57-67).* In addition, a methacholine challenge is relatively insensitive and has a high false-negative rate *(Project S.E.N.S.O.R. News. Michigan State University-College of Human Medicine. Volume 10, No. 2. Spring 1999).*

CASE FOUR

ALLEGED POST SURGICAL HEPATITIS

M r. H was a 53 year old man with end-stage cirrhosis of the liver secondary to hepatitis C virus infection. It was his claim that he contracted hepatitis C while undergoing neck surgery in 2000 to treat a work-related injury. He was therefore claiming that a liver transplant was necessary to treat a medical condition arising out of a work-related injury. The issue in this case is whether or not Mr. H's hepatitis C infection was caused by a blood transfusion during his work-related operation in the year 2000.

The peer-reviewed medical literature indicated that the risk of being infected with hepatitis C virus during the course of a blood transfusion after 1992 approaches zero.

"The introduction of second-generation anti-HCV assays has reduced the frequency of transfusion-associated hepatitis C to almost imperceptible levels, 1 in 100,000."

Harrison's Principles of Internal Medicine. Fifteenth Edition. Copyright 2001. The McGraw-Hill Companies, Inc. ISBN 0-07-007272-8. Page 1729.

Mr. H had an appendectomy in 1965. During that time period the risk of infection with hepatitis C virus was relatively high.

"During the 1970s, the likelihood of acquiring hepatitis after transfusion of voluntarily donated, HBsAg-screened blood was approximately 10% per patient (up to 0.9% per unit transfused); 90 to 95% of these cases were classified, based on serologic exclusion of hepatitis A and B, as "non-A, non-B" hepatitis. For patients requiring transfusion of pooled products, such as clotting factor concentrates, the risk was even higher, up to 20 to 30%, while for those receiving such products as albumin and immune globulin, because of prior treatment of these materials by heating to 60ºC or cold ethanol fractionation, there was no risk of hepatitis."

Harrison's Principles of Internal Medicine. Fifteenth Edition. Copyright 2001. The McGraw-Hill Companies, Inc. ISBN 0-07-007272-8. Page 1729.

He also had a history of having experimented with intravenous drugs.

"A history of injection drug use, even in the remote past, is of great importance in assessing the risk for hepatitis B and C. Injection drug use is now the single most common risk factor for hepatitis C. Transfusion with blood or blood products is no longer and important risk factor for acute viral hepatitis. However, blood transfusions received before the introduction of sensitive enzyme immunoassays for antibody to hepatitis C virus (anti-HCV) in 1992 is an important risk factor for chronic hepatitis C."

Harrison's Principles of Internal Medicine. Fifteenth Edition. Copyright 2001. The McGraw-Hill Companies, Inc. ISBN 0-07-007272-8. Page 1709.

The risk of having developed a hepatitis C virus infection in 2000 when Mr. H had his surgery to treat a work-related condition was 1 case in 100,000 transfusions. This represents an extremely low risk of infection. However, the risk of contracting hepatitis C during an intra-operative blood transfusion in 1965 was high. In addition, intravenous drug use placed him at high risk of contracting a hepatitis C virus infection. Consequently, given the extremely low risk of developing hepatitis C during a blood transfusion in 2000 and the high risk represented by his past history, the cause of his hepatitis C and cirrhosis of the liver was not his surgery for a work-related injury.

CASE FIVE

RADIUM EXPOSURE

M r. R is a 51-year-old man who was employed as an operating engineer of heavy equipment. He was working at the site of an abandoned watch factory. The factory was an old facility that was approximately one hundred years old that had a long history of manufacturing watch faces and dials. The EPA was involved in mandating the clean-up of the facility. The factory building had been demolished approximately one year previously. Mr. R was operating an excavator with a forty thousand pound hammer breaking concrete on the site when the hammer suddenly broke through the concrete into an underground tank. A milky pink liquid splashed out of the tank onto his face, arms, body, and legs. His clothing was soaked with the pink liquid. The liquid also got into his eyes causing burning of the eyes and skin. When he descended from the equipment, he slipped on demolished hardwood flooring that was covered by the pink liquid. This caused numerous splinters of wood in both hands. He then left the job site to return to the camp grounds where he was staying. At the camp grounds he showered and changed his clothing. His skin continued to burn even after showering and changing his clothing. He returned to the work site that evening and noticed that the boom on the machinery he was operating when he was splashed with the pink liquid was glowing in the dark with a greenish blue color.

The next morning he had a reddish discoloration of his skin and hives on his skin. The skin rash continued with the addition, approximately a month later, of blisters. At about the same time, he began suffering extreme redness of the sclera of his eyes. He sought attention from an ophthalmologist and was referred to the ophthalmology service at a university medical center. Despite intensive medical attention to his eyes, his vision deteriorated to the point of legal blindness. He is currently legally blind and depends upon his family for assistance in activities of daily living.

He has no past medical history of hypertension, diabetes mellitus, heart disease, pulmonary disease including asthma, gastrointestinal disease, renal disease, endocrine disease, connective tissue disease, or disease of the nervous system. He also has no past history of syphilis. A scar that developed on his lower leg after the above mentioned spill has undergone malignant transformation and has been treated.

He has no known allergies.

His only mediation is 1% prednisolone acetate ophthalmic suspension and occasion Vicodin for skin pain.

His mother is 71 years old and is in good health. His father is 80 and is in good health other than having had a minor stroke. He has three sisters who are in good health. He has two sons and two daughters who are in good health.

He does smoke about three or four cigarettes each day. He has only rarely consumed alcohol. He was heavily engaged in athletic activities as a child and as a young man. He is married and lives in a single-family home with his wife and three of his children. He has a couple of dogs. He began work as an operating engineer shortly after high school. He worked for a short time in a bakery company making cookies.

Review of systems was non-contributory other than back pain and numbness and tingling in his feet.

Physical examination showed a well nourished, well developed man in no acute distress. He is blind and needs to be lead when walking. Examination of the ears, nose and throat was normal. He had extreme photophobia so that an examination of the fundi of the eyes was not possible. There was slight erythema of the sclera of the eyes. His neck was supple without bruits or mass. Lungs were clear to auscultation. Heart had a regular rate and rhythm. Abdomen had positive bowel sounds in all four quadrants. There was no abdominal tenderness or rigidity. Extremities were without edema or cyanosis. Cranial nerves II through XII were intact. There were no gross motor or sensory deficits. Reflexes were normal and symmetrical bilaterally. His skin showed irregular flat whitish scars on the face, chest, arms, and legs. A review of medical records shows that he has been diagnosed with bilateral iridocyclitis with possible panuveitis since his chemical exposure.

OPINION

In my opinion, Mr. R suffered an exposure to a radium containing material when he was splashed with the pink liquid at the site of the old abandoned watch factory. The use of radium in watch face manufacturing is well known.

"Radium was the first demonstrable radioactive carcinogen. One of the first industrial uses of radium was in the manufacture of luminous paint. Mixing powdered Ra with ZnS crystals causes the crystals to glow because of their absorption of energy from alpha particles emitted by the radium. Luminous paint

made in this way was applied to clocks and scientific instrument dials by women who pointed the paint brushes between their lips to achieve fine lines. Minute amounts of radium were swallowed each time that the brush was pointed. In the early 1920s, several dial painters were found to be suffering from degeneration of the jawbone. Follow-up studies uncovered more cases of bone damage, including osteogenic sarcoma, among the radium dial painters and definitely established radium as the etiological agent. Further studies on radium dial painters and on patients who had been treated medically with injections of radium confirmed the carcinogenicity of radium. "

Hamilton & Hardy's Industrial Toxicology. Fifth Edition. © 1998 Mosby-Year Book, Inc. IBSN—08151-4181-5. Pages 509-510.

Radiation is well known to be able to cause chorioretinal degeneration.

Sefau SO, Dorey MW, Brownstein S, Romanchuk K, Little JM, Chisholm IA.

Radiation-induced chorioretinal degeneration: a clinicopathological report of three cases.

Can J Opthalmol. 2003 Feb;38(1):57-62.

BACKGROUND: *With the shift in radiotherapy towards the posterior segment and with the use of lead screens to shield the anterior segment, posterior segment lesions have become more readily recognized. The purpose of this study is to highlight the effects of ionizing radiation on the choroids and to demonstrate how this can result in visual loss, particularly if the macula is involved.* METHODS: *Histopatholgical study of three enucleated eyes of three patients who had received ionizing radiation: a 27-year-old woman who had received radiation as a child for a hemangioma of the left side of the face, a 16-year-old girl who had received radiation at age 11 years for a malignant mesenchymoma of the right maxillia, and a 4-year-old girl who had received radiation at age 1 year for a retinoblastoma of the right eye.* RESULTS: *Histopathological examination of the three globes showed extensive chorioretinal degeneration, among other ocular findings. In all cases the fellow eye did not show similar chorioretinal lesions. As all three patients were relatively young, the degree of chorioretinal degeneration was considered to be secondary to radiation treatment.* INTERPRETATION: *Vascular damage from ionizing radiation is not limited to the retina. It can also affect the choroids in the form of chorioretinal degeneration. Since most of the intraocular circulation arises from the uveal vessels, chorioretinal degenerative lesions may be extensive and may even involve the macula.*

The fact that the pink liquid glowed in the dark with a greenish-blue color and that it came from an underground tank on the site of an old watch factory is strong evidence the liquid contained radium. The fact that Mr. R's visual changes and skin changes began shortly after his having been splashed with the pinkish liquid is evidence that the liquid is the cause of his visual and skin changes. Radiation exposure is well known to cause the type of ocular damage that afflicts Mr. R. The skin lesions with malignant transformation are an additional factor that strongly points to radium exposure. Consequently, it is my opinion to a reasonable degree of medical certainty that Mr. R's ocular and skin conditions were caused by a workplace radium exposure while on the site of the abandoned watch factory.

A CASE OF LIGHTNING AND CARPAL TUNNEL SYNDROME

M s. Z is a 50-year-old woman that claimed to have developed carpal tunnel syndrome due to a lightning strike. In 1998, she was a passenger in a pick-up truck driven by her husband, when it was struck by lightning. She claims that lightning struck the antenna of a citizen band radio on the truck, causing a rear tire to blow out. She also claims that she was holding a Styrofoam™ cup of coffee in her lap with both of her hands at the time of the lightning strike. The car ended up in a ditch after the lightning strike.

There are a number of problems concerning Mr. Z's claim of having developed carpal tunnel syndrome due to the lightning strike.

The first problem is that there is no evidence that she suffered any burns due to the lightning strike. Burns are frequently found at the exit point of the electrical current in electrocution. This does not appear to have happened to Ms. Z.

The second problem is that Ms. Z was holding a Styrofoam™ cup containing coffee at the time of the lightning strike. Styrofoam™ is a trademark for a light, resilient polystyrene plastic which has excellent electrical insulating properties *(The Merck Index, Eleventh Edition. Merck & Co. 1989. Page 1397)*. Since electrical current follows the path of least resistance, electrical energy should not have flowed to her hands even if she were exposed to electrical current as a result of the lightning strike.

The third problem is that an electromyogram (EMG) showed no denervation in either of the upper extremities. While there were some changes on the EMG suggesting a possible myopathic problem, they were the opposite of post-lightning changes described in the medical literature.

The fourth and most serious problem is that the lightning strike occurred while Ms. Z was a passenger in a metal skinned truck. While it is possible for lightning to strike a motor vehicle, one of the safest places to be during a lighting storm is in an enclosed metal motor vehicle. The reason for this is that when a metal motor vehicle is struck by lighting, the electrical current flows in the metal skin of the motor vehicle and not into the occupants of the vehicle. The metal motor vehicle acts as a "Faraday cage" that is impenetrable to the electrical current *(Cherington M. Lightning and Transportation. Semin Neurol 1995 Dec;15(4):362-366).* The fact that her husband was holding the steering wheel at the time of the lightning strike and was not injured or killed is a strong demonstration of the effect of a Faraday cage.

Therefore, it is highly unlikely that the lightning strike caused her carpal tunnel syndrome. She was almost certainly not exposed to electrical current from the lightning strike because of the action of the truck as a Faraday cage. The most likely cause of her carpal tunnel syndrome, was cumulative trauma from prior employment, including scrubbing tires at her husband's whitewall tire cleaning company.

BIBLIOGRAPHY

Curtis D. Klaassen. Casarett and Doull's Toxicology. The Basic Science of Poisons. Sixth Edition. 2001. McGraw-Hill. New York.

Raymond D. Harbison. Hamilton & Hardy's Industrial Toxicology. Fifth Edition. 1998. Mosby. St. Louis.

Peter J. Baxter. Hunter's Diseases of Occupations. Ninth Edition. 2000. Arnold. London.

Gerald W. Boston and M. Stuart Madden. Law of Environmental and toxic torts: Cases, Materials and Problems. 1994 West Publishing Co. St. Paul.

Jean Macchiaroli Eggen. Toxic Torts in a Nutshell. 1995. West Publishing Co. St. Paul.

Made in the USA
Middletown, DE
16 July 2024

57368682R00104